Zerilda's Chair
And Other Poems

GEORGE De GREGORIO

©2009 George De Gregorio

ISBN: 978-0-557-18048-6

Editor: Mark Fogarty

Covers: Steven De Gregorio

WHITE CHICKENS PRESS

PO Box 1691

Rutherford NJ 07070

For additional copies:

www.lulu.com/content/7857779

Table of Contents

AUTHOR's NOTE: FOOD FOR THE SOUL

When my family and I moved to Rutherford, N.J., in 1961 so I could take a job with *The New York Times*, I would occasionally see an elderly man on Park Avenue, the town's main business street, walking to the library or stopping in one of the stores there. He was pointed out to me as Dr. Williams, the retired pediatrician, but I knew he was a noted poet as well.

I never had the occasion to meet William Carlos Williams, who died in 1963, just a couple of years after I moved to the borough. But I wish I had, because when I came to the end of my career for *The Times* after 39 years as an editor, I began to write poetry, and I'm sure I could have benefited from any advice he might have given me.

I have never taken a college course on how to write poetry, but it was in college that I learned to appreciate its beauty. So, in essence, my work is self-taught and my subject matter stems from the everyday, mundane happenings which have crossed my path or have lodged secretly in my brain. If I sometimes seem out of my realm, blame it on inexperience or an ego reaching too far. Whatever, I have tried to be sincere in my presentations and selections.

I have a deep prejudice in favor of and a deep appreciation for poetry. I lean toward the old masters – Shakespeare, Whitman, Wordsworth, Yeats, Keats, Auden, Eliot and, of course, Dr. Williams, our own wise hometown man-of-letters. That is not to say, I don't have a deep appreciation, as well, for the young poets of our generation, and the generations to come.

I believe poetry is food for the soul; that a person, or a country, which does not tap the rich vein of its poetic nature, is depriving itself of spiritual inquisitiveness and sustenance. It is losing touch with the thread which can knit us all into one fabric, capable of creating a peaceful, understanding and loving world.

4

The poems in *Zerilda's Chair and Other Poems* are an attempt at picking up little pieces and fitting them into a semblance of something whole and meaningful. They go back in time to before World War II, and right up to the present day, remembering such things as baseball games played in the ardent rush of youth, an adventurous summer as a young man in Montana, the winos who worked in the industrial mills nearby who would buy cheap clothes at the Army-Navy surplus store for their weekends on the town. And they remember the most extraordinary times of my life, the special occasions of family life, my emotional reunion with my brother when he came back safe from World War II, the heartbreak when a family friend did not come back from Iraq.

I could not have done it alone. I have many to thank for their help: my wife, Barbara, of course, has been my constant advisor extraordinaire; Jane Fisher, the director of the Rutherford Public Library, who wrote the Foreword, and opened the door for me to the William Carlos Williams Poetry Cooperative Second Wednesday readings; John Trause, the poet and WCW cooperative coordinator; Jim Klein, noted poet and retired college professor and teacher of poetry; Mark Fogarty, the insightful editor and publisher of this volume; Steven De Gregorio, my son, and designer of the covers, and the rest of my family, Barry, Karen and Carl, who gave me constant encouragement.

Also the folks at the WCW Red Wheelbarrow Poets Workshop, led by Mr. Klein, whose talented and keen eyes oversaw virtually all these poems and offered their thumbs up or thumbs down. I would also like to acknowledge the editors at the journals where some of these poems first appeared: *The Rutherford Red Wheelbarrow* and *Three Quarks Daily*.

GEORGE DE GREGORIO, Rutherford, N.J. 2009

Foreword: Exploring That Which Is The Smallest and the Biggest in Ourselves

Rutherford, N.J. has recently been the site of a remarkable poetry revival. Spearheaded by George De Gregorio and a handful of other local poets, this revival followed on the heels of a major William Carlos Williams Poetry Symposium, held in 2005 at the local arts center named for Doc Williams, Rutherford's resident poet-doctor. Today, retired newspaperman, former *New York Times* editor, man-of-letters, and Rutherfordian George De Gregorio is a co-founder of the WCW Poetry Collaborative of Southern Bergen County and Poet Laureate of *The Red Wheelbarrow*, a group of poets that gathers for weekly workshops and hosts readings in Rutherford and other venues around North Jersey and New York.

It has been my good fortune to hear George recite many of the poems in this beautiful collection at local poetry readings since the launch of the poetry collaborative in 2006. So as I read the manuscript of *Zerilda's Chair and Other Poems* to prepare this Foreword, I heard George's thoughtful, measured voice ringing through in each piece. Whether or not you have had the opportunity to know George and hear him read his poems, you will no doubt become quickly engaged by the freshness of his ideas, his carefully crafted sentences, and his beautiful use of language.

For George, writing poems came after his retirement from *The Times*. "The poems started coming," he said, "when I felt the need to occupy myself with those questions of who am I, why I'm here, and what are the ideas in life?" He goes on to say, "as I got older, there was no one telling me what I ought to do, what I ought to be, and so I was crazy enough to act like a poet." While writing poetry may have come later in life, George has been reading the great poets since he was a boy.

Yeats, Wordsworth, Auden, and Whitman are among those he considers favorites. "I've always loved to read them aloud," he said. "I enjoy the novelists, but to be a great poet is a gift. I think any novelist would give his right arm to be a poet, for it is poetry that gives us the freedom to explore that which is the smallest and the biggest in ourselves."

And it is a great poet that we discover here in this comprehensive body of work. Not unlike WCW, the "everyday stuff" and the "average scene" are at the core of George's poetry. The ideas are what's in us, the emotions nuanced, and the language accessible. This work catches the eye and penetrates the psyche. His Red Wheelbarrow poet colleagues concur — George is a dignified public poet, taking on issues of interest to both the real world and the world of letters.

Zerilda's Chair and Other Poems depicts the souls of everyday people. The places are described vividly and efficiently, transporting us "there" at once where we can almost catch a whiff of the odors that linger in the kitchen, on the family porch, on the streets of Nantucket, or under the first leaves of a spring tree. Many of the poems are reminiscent of simpler times — penny candy and sand castles and thirty-five cent movies — but never sappy, nor overly sentimental. Other pieces deliver on the ubiquity of the modern — bottled water, email, discount store grand-openings, and cell phones. A salute to the role of the arts, our sports heroes, and the Boss, Bruce Springsteen, rounds out the volume.

We're treated to caring and supportive words about the craft of poetry writing and the poetry community that George helps create and continues to nurture in both "The Workshop" and "To the Young Poets." Celebrating the poets that have influenced his own life, George beckons: Wake up, Walt Whitman! / Wake up, William Carlos Williams! / Don't laugh Walt! / Don't laugh Carlos! / Your poetic clout still keeps America singing ("Reveille for Two Poets"). And in "Let the

Words Bleed," George says, "Writing poems is hard lonely work, like this one, started yesterday." Indeed.

In *Zerilda's Chair and Other Poems*, we hear the voice of experience from a poet who knows a thing or two about this world, but one humble enough to recognize that there is always more to learn. We see that some folks travel through life easily, with privilege, while others struggle for acceptance. George takes up the challenging issues of the twentieth century: anti-Semitism, racism, aging, politics, and war deaths find a place in his work.

Perhaps most striking are the images of places that might be charming enough on their own — rooms with striped wallpaper like peppermint candy ("Rooms"), and the double high windows in Mrs. Palmieri's kitchen ("Eight-Foot Ceilings") — but in the end leave us feeling vaguely uncomfortable, mindful. Nor does George shy away from sharing his own emotions. Words written for his children, his wife, acknowledge that relationships require sweat, tears, and commitment, and that above all, love is the greatest force.

In his poem "Same Old Story," George writes, "There is no magic wand to help construct vivid, real and coherent sentences." Yet readers of these poems may well think the poet possesses just such a magic wand. Which brings us to the title poem, "Zerilda's Chair." Who is Zerilda anyway, and what of her chair? She was the poet's mother-in-law, an athletic, outspoken woman with some spunk! George has inherited her chair, has had it restored, and describes how it becomes magical for him. "I fall asleep there and I wake fully revived," he told me. It seems that Zerilda's chair is, in part, the magic wand that helped inspire the writer to assemble this masterful collection of poems. Fellow readers will surely join me in wishing George continued success exploring that which is the smallest and the biggest in ourselves.

JANE FISHER, Director, Rutherford Public Library

All the World's a Stage

AMERICA, THE BEAUTIFUL

The last best hope for man on Earth, which Whitman lovingly said would be blessed with big, bright, booming days, where he walked the bloody battlefields and wept over the graves of the Civil War's gallant dead, has once again seen the arm of spiritual decay descend upon it and threaten ruin.

Wall Street's swollen head, pressing out with petulance and greed, has overstepped its bounds, and with help from drowsy-eyed Congressmen, unable or unwilling to see the gathering storm, has put the nation once again at risk.

Foreclosures, a symbol of 1930s' despair, have sprouted again, banks have collapsed, businesses, large and small, are in peril, joblessness grows by record leaps, sales are dropping and the average family is beleaguered, confused and fearful of what tomorrow may bring.

The gyrating and spiraling stock market, daily puts investors and pensioners in danger. Barack Obama, the first black man to be elected President of the United States, has won the right and responsibility to steer the nation's ship in the wake of a steep financial crisis and wars on two fronts. He would be wise to ask for guidance, not only from the experts, but also from the hand of the Almighty.

Automotive C.E.O.s at Chrysler and General Motors, hat in hand, plead and persuade Congress to lend them billions in bailouts to save their businesses, once the envy of the world, now limp and fearful and fallen into bankruptcy. Bread lines, soup kitchens, men selling apples on street corners, thankfully, have not come into view. There are no soul singers like Woody Guthrie to rouse and soothe the people with words which remind them of who they are and assure them that they have a vested interest in the fruited plains.

"This land is your land,
This land is my land,
This land was made for
you and me."

ZERILDA'S CHAIR

They brought back the chair the other day
and you wouldn't believe it – a resurrection,
a transformation, a restoration.
The old wing back left to us by the mother
of my wife, the woman named Zerilda,
who skated as a young girl on the mill ponds
of Massachusetts with Olympian skill
and the graceful figure that a budding movie star might envy.
It was the flapper age when bobbed hairstyles were in vogue.
How was she to know she carried
the same name as the mother of Jesse James?

The chair was the thing!
I like to think it was bequeathed to me,
just me, by this woman who endured the stings
of six brothers and a sister with a handicapped arm.
The over-used chair, taken from our home
like a corpse, worn down to the bone,
the wood frame showing through the fabric,
scuffed as if a dozen mice had eaten it.

The upholsterer said: "Well, let's see,
it'll need a lot of work. Don't know if it's worth restoring."
If Zerilda had been alive,
she would have had a quick retort.
"Brother, this chair has been through hell
and the Great Depression so don't give us any lip.
Just get on with it."

The refurbished chair took center stage,
with new adornments of teal-blue dotted fabric
looking like a brilliant night sky
with a million twinkling stars.

It was restuffed for me to lounge in my bedroom,
to tie my shoes and pull up my socks, to snooze,
to snuggle with my wife, or to help break a fall
while undressing for bed in the dark
with a load on after a late night out.

But my thoughts always went back to Zerilda,
who had bought the chair years ago at auction.
She had withstood tough times with a shrug and a laugh,
traits which brushed off on her children
and gave them strength of character.
"Hey girl," an admiring voice rang out from nowhere.
"Unlace those skates, and get a move on.
We've got places to go."
For Zerilda, those places would be
unseen and far away, unheard of,
a new world where the stings
of the old one were washed away,
left to those who dared not dream
of frozen skating ponds
and regal chairs of velvet and gold.

COAL TOWN

O holy night
immaculate
product
of a needy
world
begging
for a sign
to come out
of the weary soil
where men
dig
for coal
in the craggy
mountains
of Pennsylvania
bituminous
anthracite
in the bowels
of darkness
and defamation
free but not free
bound by need
even tradition
sons and daughters
families
doggedly
inhaling
the lung-infesting air
that kills
still
they toil
until
they surface
in the glaring

beneficent sun
a new day
spent
but not beaten
a new dawn
nudges a sign
an omen
that something
magical
is about to happen
fear and despair
are set aside
but much
remains the same
breathing
coal dust
still kills
new hope
and strength
emerge
from the warmth
of nearby towns
smoke
swirls
from
housetops
the movements
of sexy
young girls
their thighs
bulging
with heat
make appetites
swell
and rewards
for hard work

are within reach
all is calm
all is bright
O holy night
pervasive grime
is washed away
soon
for a brief time
the air is clean
enough
to breathe
and the direction
of the night
becomes
straight and pristine
starry and sublime
O holy night

CHRISTMAS IN PORTLAND, OREGON 2008

Snow in front of you,
snow to the left,
snow to the right,
snow everywhere.

Into this cauldron of whiteness
many descended after thousands of miles
aloft for an inordinate amount of time,
to be where so much snow
had not fallen in 100 years,
and spurred by the timeless urge
to join in the spirit of Christmas.

My eldest son's home, on a street
appropriately named Rex Street,
was the beacon, a virtual
wonderland of snow and trees
and decorations, a path leading
the way to a blessed family reunion.

Snow in front of you,
snow to the left,
snow to the right,
snow everywhere.

All came together, sons and daughters,
grandchildren, grandparents, uncles, aunts,
nieces, nephews, parents, friends,
an outpouring of love, with the peace
of a manger scene, as if multiples of the three kings,
in jeans and boots, and bearing gifts,
had found a place, at last, to hang out
and take a load off their feet.

GEORGE DE GREGORIO

Snow in front of you,
snow to the left,
snow to the right,
snow everywhere.

The dinner of seven fish courses rolled out,
sating every appetite, and keeping
the holy tradition one more time.
All the cooking and stuff was done
by my son Barry and his legions of sous chefs,
with 21 guests, another multiple of three,
enjoying cuisine and wine equal to, if not better than,
any served at a high-priced New York bistro.

All in attendance braved the onslaught
of the most brutal snow storm to visit
the Pacific Northwest in nearly a century,
taking uncertain flights from New York,
New Jersey, Pennsylvania, Florida, Los Angeles,
Los Gatos, Calif., and by car from local areas,
traveling over treacherous, snow-packed, icy roads.

Snow in front of you,
snow to the left,
snow to the right,
snow everywhere.

It was as if all had followed a star,
like a North Star, which brought them to a place
of warmth and commemoration
where, in their presence, too, was Sean Fennerty,
the son and brother who was killed in Iraq,
sacrificing his life for freedom.

They had all come together this night
to celebrate the birth of One,

whose act of sacrifice illuminated
a world shrouded in darkness –
a world thirsting
for the milk and honey of human kindness.

Snow in front of you,
snow to the left,
snow to the right,
snow everywhere.

FUGITIVE BEAUTY

The term "fugitive beauty" came
to me in a letter. A friend's wife
had used it in conversation. My friend
is a painter who studied in Paris.
I sought his opinion on poetry.

Fugitive beauty, evanescent, fleeting,
as if it implied a criminality
I did not understand.
Did all art start that way –
alone, furtive, so coiled
in its incubation that it feared
possible success or failure?

Fugitive, running away,
not standing with the norm, the herd,
not strong enough
to be judged?

Or did it mean beauty as Keats meant it?
"Truth is beauty, beauty truth" –
a raw truth, or a new dimension of beauty,
a new adjective
to describe eagles soaring,
no parameters,
like prisoners breaking out.

Out there by itself,
not great, not mediocre,
but flying in its own space
against all normalcy, blasting off
to its own truthfulness,
its own freedom.

RETIREMENT

You'd be surprised how many people
want to tell you how to spend your time
when you hang up your well-worn spikes.
They're downright indecent and gauche.

You'd think they'd have the decency
to let a fellow make up his own mind.
Off the bat, they've got you volunteering,
prodding to do good deeds.

Driving old ladies to doctors' appointments
is their idea of being a well-meaning scout.
Don't they know if I were to drive a lady anywhere
it certainly wouldn't be to a doctor's office.

Or how about volunteering to help out
at a hospital, surrounding yourself with illness
and pain and suffering just to prove to the world
you have an unlimited capacity for compassion?

Maybe I'd like to spend a day at the ball park
watching Jeter scoop up grounders at shortstop,
or take in an exciting movie, or read a good book.
It seems they mean well, but they don't get it.

I always thought retirement should be for doing
whatever pleases you best, provided you didn't
harm anyone and you had ample health and funds.
If you add it all up it comes out even.

After all, what do we really want out of life?
The poet said "a loaf of bread, a jug of wine and thou."
That sounds reasonable, and yet we hold out,
not knowing how much or how little we will need.

CHRISTMAS TREE

It was ordered from Oregon where trees,
like Frasers, are supposed to be without peer.
They are a little pricey,
but the company that sells them
is known to stand behind its products.
We trusted that it would be delivered
on time for the holiday and in good shape.
After all, shipping a 6-footer 3,000 miles
is daunting stuff even for FedEx.
Scheduled to arrive in two days, this charmer
took its sweet time, reaching our home in eight.
Dead on arrival!
Unwrapped, you might say, it looked
like a baby in swaddling clothes.
Our anxious home was finally calmed.
We nursed it and brought it back to life.
It had taken enough abuse.
Even before we complained,
the senders knew they had screwed up.
We doctored the tree, with drink
and a few deft cuts of the trunk and branches.
The old stand we had in the attic
thrust it upright, ready to take on lights and decorations,
and become part of a loving household.
After all, a Christmas tree, wherever it comes from,
no matter how far or how long it takes,
is entitled, with dignity and respect,
to a place at the table,
free ro spread its good cheer
to one and all,
the way Nature intended.

MRS. DENITSOVA
She stands there, feet firmly planted, immovable,
projecting strength and confidence, even beauty.
A masseuse, this little one plies her Belarusian hands
and fingers as if kneading dough for the bread of life.

Maya, once a nurse in the old country, is the main cog,
the force that guided her family to the shores
of the new country, as if thrust by the hand of God,
into a bustling, vibrant society filled with possibilities.

The first days were the hardest, trudging five miles
through snow each day to her job at the Jewish Y.
Night school to learn English, then community college
and classes among strangers with strange ideas.

Friendly and determined, she was quick to learn
of credit cards, new cars and part-time jobs,
home ownership, finger-nail salons and Best Buy stores.
Making and spending money could even be fun!

It was hard, but necessary, to leave behind days of poor pay,
not enough food, and anti-Semitic taunts.
Now, if her son, Alex, wanted to study to be a rabbi, so be it.
The door was open, no barriers stood in the way.

It was hardest for Valery, her husband, who spoke no English.
Work was hard to find and he learned about unemployment.
Her daughter, Anna, went to business college and worked
selling leather coats in a tony store at the big mall.

And so the long journey of one more immigrant family
to America came full circle.
Citizenship became a reality for the whole family.
Once again, the promise was kept:
"Give me your tired, your poor, your huddled masses…"

MRS. COHEN

Mrs. Cohen used to say she could make a meal
out of a cup of coffee, a hard roll and butter.
She and her son ran the Army and Navy store where
she altered the pants for the winos on Saturday night.

An odd bunch the winos, they worked hard in factories
and came in to spruce up like newly-minted Beau Brummels:
a pair of $2.50 jeans, a $1.29 shirt and a pair of 29-cent socks
and they would feel fresh and free and ready to paint the town.

Mrs. Cohen worried that the winos should wash their old clothes;
poor folks, she said, should practice frugality and not squander
funds on booze, women and galavanting about town.
She worried about her other son
who was a lawyer and was in the war.

Trains passed on the tracks outside the back room
where she altered the pants and saw troops
and tanks heading for the fighting.
She and her son read the papers and followed the war every day
and worried about the safety of her other son who was in Italy.

Mrs. Cohen continued to say she could make a meal
out of a cup of coffee, a hard roll and butter
as if she thought of that repast, not for its meagerness,
but as sort of a ritual -- a sacrifice good for the soul.

One day a Western Union telegram was delivered to Mrs. Cohen.
Her son Isaac read it: The War Department regrets
that your son Nathan has been killed in action at Anzio
"It cannot be," she cried in disbelief, "it cannot be."

It took a long time for Mrs. Cohen to accept her son's death.
Her visage was always sad now and her face had aged,

and in ordinary daily tasks and chats with neighbors,
she never again mentioned how she could make a meal
out of a cup of coffee, a hard roll and butter.

IF YOU HAVEN'T ANYTHING TO SAY

If you haven't anything to say,
there is no reason to force it.
You might be happier giving up the idea,
using your time for something else.
You might get more satisfaction
digging a ditch than racking your brain,
trying to describe an ultimate truth.
Too often, you can be lost in grandiose ideas,
when all you need is a simple statement of fact.

GEORGE DE GREGORIO

A FEW RANDOM THOUGHTS

Tell me, what did I say to you that day
on the steps of the library, where you worked
and I visited so often you might have thought
I was hanging around, looking to make out?

It was before I left school for good after graduation.
Did I stun you? You looked so baffled,
as if the suddenness of our meeting gave you pause.
I was surprised, too; the way you looked made me curious.

You were wearing a blue jacket and skirt,
with a white blouse open at the neck,
stuff you once told me you had made.
I had seen you wearing the outfit before.

You were good at making clothes,
and had an eye for quality things.
You said you made them to avoid
buying inferior materials that cheapened

your look and appearance, which was always just right –
fashionable, despite being hand-tailored.
We made no promises and you wished me luck
with my writing. I wished you luck, too,

with your dream of going to New York
to become a high-fashion buyer.
God knows you were the only one
to wish me luck about my future.

Where I came from, writing was a wild dream.
So I went off to Montana to get started, I thought,
on the great American novel.
I had just finished a two-week session

25

at the university's writers' conference.
I had won a scholarship and got encouragement
from Malcolm Cowley, a famous critic
who had read my prize-winning work.

He was an expert on Hemingway
and a close friend
of William Carlos Williams,
the doctor and famous poet.

NIGHTTIME

Cascading darkness
drapes the twilight hours,
daylight is obliterated.
Nighttime!

Romance,
apprehension,
caution.
prowlers,
sleepwalkers,
dreamers.

A touch of Champagne,
a step or two
on the dance floor.
The bliss
of a kiss.
Nighttime!

The end of a perfect day!

EARMARKS

America's pure-breds
     -- 535 strong –
men and women

  privileged,

elected to make the laws

from smoky
      mountains, steaming streets.
  cities large and small,

chiseled gerrymandered districts,
    thick ethic masses –

Latinos, Asians Blacks, Irish, Italians, Poles, Jews,

    --EARMARKS! –

    legal and illegal,

    from border states, coast lines
flanked by oceans,

       dandies, upstarts, college-trained,
           devious manipulators of flesh and money,
graft and fraud.

     magicians
         of high quality and low,
   nurtured
from peasant wombs

suckled financiers,

misbegotten bankers.

Catholics, Protestants, Adventists.

Where are they taking us?

Southerners still flashing
rebel flags,

clinging
to segregationist ideals.

Northerners

smug in Ivy-covered
class rooms,

doomed from here

to Eternity. . .

Where are they taking us?

What have they in store for us?

Has the electorate really voted them in?

How do we
get them out?

Are they leading us down

the fun-house corridors

with mirrors reflecting

their fat bellies and baggy pants?

Are the women immune
    because they are women,

    or have they caught-on
to the masculine game?

Ride the commissary car,
coffee and donuts everyone.

The Treasury has a trillion
    to dispense, 20 billion here,
20 billion there. 20 billion

everywhere!

Do not mention names,
    everyone's to blame.

In the corridors of fame,
there is no one to proclaim

the intentions of a righteous few,
    for all have tasted

the bitter herb

  of corruption,

    and let it go at that.

EIGHT-FOOT CEILINGS

Mrs. Palmieri's apartment had five large rooms
with ceilings eight feet tall and double windows just as big.

In the spring, she liked to clean the mammoth rooms,
put up fresh curtains, and relax on the veranda.

But the ceilings were too high so she hired Julius,
a colored man who did windows for a few bucks.

Her neighbors didn't exactly like her hiring Julius.
Mrs. Fantone said she'd boil the dishes Julius ate from

and that Mrs. Palmieri, a widow, should know better
than to hire a Negro and upset the neighborhood.

Mrs. Palmieri laid out a plain meal for Julius
and admired the way he used the knife and fork.

"Thank you, ma'am," he said when she paid him,
 "I'm much obliged," "My pleasure," Mrs. Palmieri said.

DOUBLE OR NOTHING

I'm as old now as Grandfather was
when he and Grandmother came to live with us
during the Great Depression.
Our family grew from five to seven in a flash
and my brothers and I learned
what sharing meant.

Grandfather lost all his hair when he entered
middle age and he cultivated his baldness
with a kind of nobleman's demeanor.
He dressed in white shirt, vest and tie every day,
with suspenders to boot –
although he had no work or job to go to.

The previous year he had lost his broom factory:
everybody must have swept away
their good luck from the front porch
that New Year's Eve – you couldn't sell a broom.
But Grandfather kept his sense of humor.

He would cajole me into playing the forehead game.
Out of his vest pocket came a nickel.
"It's yours," he'd say, "if I can't flip it
and make it land on my forehead and not slip off."
"O.K.," I'd say "but no changing the rules,
like two out of three times if you miss the first time."

Grandfather flipped the coin high over his head.
It grazed his forehead and fell to the floor.
He did this four more times, until I had amassed
the enormous sum of 25 cents -- all mine
to buy whatever I wanted.

Then he forked over the coins and said:
"One more time, double or nothing, O.K.?"
My eyes grew greener and I took on the bet.
Grandfather let the next nickel fly.
It seemed to stay in the air
for an eternity, finally landing flat on his forehead
and staying there as if it were glued to the skin.

"Gee, how did you do that?" I said.
"Nothing to it, I could have done it every time."
Disappointment spanned my face
as I looked down at the floor.
Grandfather noticed, and said:
"C'mon here, little one, and look in my vest pocket."
I went over to him and put my hand in his pocket.
There was a 50 cent piece in it.
"Double or nothing," Grandfather said. "That's for you."

EMAILBLEWS

deres a nu langwidg in r mist & its sendin me nutz
its lak diarrhea of de finger tips & makes no cents.

It loks mor complicated dan chinese & u'd tink
its lac of punchooation & spacin were so unikue

everybody wood be hapy wit it I dunno what skool
u got 2 go 2 2 larn dis nu spelin & centance struckture

but sure as hell I dunno anybody smart enuff
to earn a PH.D in dis kind of lingo

deres sum prety smart foks in dis bisnes & im sure
dey no what der doin but sumtime I git de feelin

dey larn it best who have notin in der noggins
in de 1st place & dats y dey're up front & ahed

of de pak when it comes 2 singin dos blewsy emailblews.

THOSE GOOD OLD SONGS

Music to our ears!
The old songs:
drooling,
in sweet nostalgic harmony.

"My Gal Sal"
"Swanee" (Did you know Gershwin wrote it?),
"Sweet Adeline",
"That Old Gang of Mine."

"Alexander's Ragtime Band"
(Written by the same Jewish immigrant
who wrote, "God Bless America"
and "White Christmas.")

You get goose bumps remembering
Alice Faye, Don Ameche, Tyrone Power.
just to name a few.
"Moonlight Bay."

They came along even before our time,
when the 20th century was prime,
and girls and boys had the time
to swoon, moon and croon.

"In My Merry Oldsmobile."
What a way to stay young.
"Hit the Road, Jack",
"I'll Be Seeing You."

Sweet was the night air
when stars were the only twinkles
in the sky and the moon
hadn't been trampled on yet.

What an age for pulling wool
over our eyes!
The price of sheet music
was cheap then.

The old piano player
cranked out the tunes,
our off-key voices tried
to stay young and gay.

We didn't know how soon
and how sadly it would all fade away
in a rumble of discordant sounds
of guns and bullets and war.

GRAND OPENING

It's like the running of the bulls in Pamplona,
when the doors swing open on the first day
and hordes of customers pour into the store,
a shiny new palace proclaiming discount heaven.

There are no traffic lights or cops to steer
the enraptured crowd so ethnically diverse
a United Nations flag could justifiably
be draped across the beckoning entrance.

What corporate genius dreamed this one up,
sitting in his swivel chair, stroking fingers in his hair,
alloting twenty-million to put cinder blocks in place
and ten-million more to stock it with cheap panache?

To be sure the global economy is being served.
Peru, Thailand, India, Italy and Brazil, to name a few,
are among the suppliers who fill the space.
In statuary, Napoleon holds sway with Beethoven.

Language tells the story: Spanish predominates
with Asian, Caribbean, African and other European
customers filling the aisles with overflowing carts
as Mom and Pop carry babies in pouches on their backs.

It's a world-scene repeated in almost every town:
a Grand Opening with free refreshments and balloons.
The cheap clothing smells of fresh dye, filling the air —
it hurts your eyes, but you'll endure it -- the price is right.
.

So we join the merry band, seeking instant satisfaction,
afraid we'll miss out if we are not first in line.
It's only junk and the sneakers are mix-and-match,
but we have endured the stampede to the Promised Land.

HENRY
Pets were never my game,
especially not for a scraggily mutt,
part snauzer, part poodle, part beagle,
energetic, like perpetual motion,
that Missy and Barry brought home
one day and he stayed for 11 years.

When I visited, he waited, perched
on the window sill
as if he had been forewarned,
ears pricked up like a rabbit's,
an inquisitive, investigative stare.
Nodding off in the wing chair,
his leap into my lap woke me;
we were old pals, bonded in love and trust.

His sixth sense bobbed up
when Missy left Raleigh
for a new job in Oregon.
That's when the bounce
went out of his legs
and he grew visibly older.

The next job in Hawaii was too much;
the mutt was left behind with Barry.
The vet said he died of congestive heart failure,
but we all knew it was from a broken heart.
He was cremated and his ashes
were kept on the mantel.

A couple of years later, there was a divorce,
and they went their separate ways.
His passing wounded and sealed our hearts:
there was never room again
for another to take his place.

LIBRARIES

My library used to be a smallish building
settled next to a big white courthouse
on a street lined with great elm trees,
a haven sitting across a beautiful green.

Three old churches bordered the green,
reminders of the 300-year-old history
of a town conceived by Pilgrim Fathers
and beckoning to the world with open arms.

My library was free, public and adequate,
though its volume of books was miniscule
compared to the millions of tomes housed
in the university, its great next-door-neighbor.

Many a summer's day was spent searching
the stacks, looking for an intellectual clue:
Saroyan, Faulkner, Twain, Fitzgerald,
Hemingway, Steinbeck, Auden.

Nowadays, you can get any title you want
at Barnes & Noble, not so different from my old public free:
quiet is observed, amid some distractions --
cafe au lait, plush chairs and bare midriffs.

Though topics change, books are immutable.
Does it really matter where you first learn
about Huck Finn and Tom Sawyer
along the great Mississippi?

While the big chain stores' cash registers ring
and best-sellers abound from politics to Pick-Up-Sticks,
the art of reading may have received a boost,
with the help of the art of merchandising.

OLD MOVIES

You have to be long in the tooth
to remember the days
when you could spend
all Sunday afternoon
in a movie house
for 35 cents,
growing up
with Mickey Mouse,
Mickey Rooney,
Popeye and Andy Hardy.
The Lone Ranger
and Fat and Skinny
who were really
Laurel and Hardy.
There were women stars, too.
Judy Garland, Ginger Rogers,
Rita Hayworth, Crawford.
Stanwyck (she came from Brooklyn).
Gable (The King), Jimmy Stewart,
Jean Arthur, Lionel Barrymore,
Spencer Tracy, MacMurray,
Edward G. Robinson, Ernie Borgnine
They were worth the 35 cents.

PASSING OF TIME

Curious eyes focused on the possible
and we dreamed of ordered and lofty things.

From the "Joy of Cooking" to Child and Beard,
our politics differed, but added the necessary spice.

Oh, 50 years is a long time by most measures
and can be riddled with angst and strife.

In good times and bad, the lessons to be learned
are sometimes lacking a good and fair teacher.

The part one plays may be large or small.
Sometimes the scales balance, sometimes they fall.

Illness came and illness went, all sustained
by faith that springtime brings new life and hope

and winter nurtures and fuels the heart
with love and loyal and lasting companionship.

GEORGE DE GREGORIO

PERFECT APRONS

At 70, they remember
each other's birthdays
with cards and Miss Pease's
sewing class when they botched
the assignment to make "perfect" aprons.

They exchange e-mail messages now,
reducing the 1,000-mile gap
that separates the old friends
in winter when Mary becomes
a snowbird in Florida.

If they could do it over again,
they probably wouldn't have botched
Miss Pease's sewing class,
but then they wouldn't
have had all the fun..

Jeannie sends a picture
or a facsimile of an apron
with her birthday card to remind
Mary of the day they messed up.

Young girls then, their joy
came from their irreverence --
no perfection for them.

So, despite their fear
of not passing the final exam
they took the penalty, stayed
after school and accepted.
a C-minus and graduated.

For over 50 years, Jeannie's card to Mary
always attached some kind of apron
as a reminder of happy days.
Straight A's and Dean's List   ·
couldn't have matched their secret joy.

ANNIVERSARY

This night I am thinking
Of many things:
Beautiful and evil.
I will always love you.

And if you will pardon me,
It is a happy thing I wish for you,
Of beautiful music,
Dance,
Rapture.

I love you very much.
In the morning,
In the daytime,
In the night.

Today,
Tomorrow,
Always.

PORCHES

If you are lucky enough to have one,
a porch is like an extra room in the house,
an extra pair of eyes looking out at the world,
a camera, seeing changing vistas,
taking candid shots, making no judgments.

A porch might be glass-enclosed or open-air,
small or large, rich and banistered,
poor or rickety, made of wood or stone,
ephemeral or full of sentiment.
A rocker, a chair or two, a swing, give comfort,
and many a romance has blossomed there.

Porches, some call them stoops, front
some of the grimiest tenements in the big cities.
or serve as welcome mats in faraway rural towns.
Porches are like lighthouses, they do not wall you in.
Mostly. they seem to be at the water's edge,
beckoning strangers and friends alike.

A porch can also be a stage
for feisty political give-and-take.
Wasn't it on a porch at Appomattox
where Grant and Lee saw eye-to-eye
and put an end to the bloody Civil War?

NANTUCKET

Before the big money people washed ashore
and Wall Street pilgrims and realtors
came to play real-life Monopoly and politics,
it was a place you could call Fantasy Island.

A place of relaxation and other worldliness,
vistas of lush mansions and overpriced cabins,
a universal place fit for beggars and kings.

A speck in the Atlantic, where Melville slept and wrote
and whalers and fishermen battled the unforgiving sea.
Peaceful now and serene, but once the vanguard
of a teeming, prosperous whaling industry.

The visitors just off the boat, debarking
into the sparkling marina, brimming
with yachts worth at least $100 million.
The cobblestones, the bandstand,

the penny candy store, the churches,
the long bicycling paths, the young girls
pedaling away, showing off
their luscious behinds. Who could forget?

A trip to Sconset, a suburb, old houses,
walking paths, beaches and rosehips,
the immutable sea pitching and tossing
as if no one existed.

Back in town, the unchanged cobblestones,
the bars and restaurants, ·
the Irish sweater shop, the bank, the benches
to comfort the elderly, all cascade

into a mosaic made by human hands
as a man plays a guitar
and sings a ditty for loose change.

HAVE I TOLD YOU LATELY

Have I told you lately that I love you?
Have I told you lately that I care?

While you dance away the hours
in the arms of another.
I am reeling in the arms of despair.

I keep thinking I am being missed
while all the while he is there.

Have I told you lately that I love you?
Have I told you lately that I care?

No use crying over spilled affections!

ROOMS

Growing up, the wallpaper in the bedroom –
blue and red streaks – looked like peppermint candy.
The memory gave you the willies,
a reminder of a carnival with barkers and freaks,
a side show of human frailty.
Nightmares stuck in your craw,
a scar seared in the brain,
a mysterious space needing identification.

The living room sported a well-worn sofa
and a Persian carpet, symbols of better days --
big holidays, farewells, weddings and birth announcements.
The kitchen spawned debates, appetites,
aromas wafting into the air; cozy and warm, earthy,
a watering hole for a jigger or two.

The attic retained battered old memories –
books, an old rocking chair, posters --
nothing so pretentious as Cairo or Tokyo or the Via Veneto.
Your rooms were serendipitous, rich and unique,
obligating you to take them with you wherever you went.
After all, weren't they among the memories
many of us cannot forget?

BOTTLED WATER

I remember lazy summer days at boys camp,
walking 15 miles to the nearby town,

counting the houses and the churches on the way,
raising such a thirst you'd fight for a drink.

If you had a nickel, it might be Coke, or soda pop,
or for free you could slurp cold water from a fountain

in the general store where they sold candy dots
on long sheets of paper for a penny.

Water in a bottle on sale was a rare thing then,
though they say Poland Spring, up there in Maine,

has been priming the pump since 1845.
That's a long stretch for building a thirst.

I don't know if those diet fellows got the bug --
water's got to be a healthy thing no matter what –

and maybe a doctor or two became an advocate
for toting Good Health's 21st-Century status symbol.

Everybody is lugging the half-liter plastic size:
teen-agers, wives, mothers, dads and brothers,

swilling it down in gyms, offices, delis and moviehouses,
quenching cotton-ball dry mouths and hangovers.

I have no flavorless grudge against the bottle.
We come into the world weaned on it, and alas,

many a tippler has foolishly succumbed to it.

GEORGE DE GREGORIO

Water is the elixir of life as bread is the staff.

All the oceans, seas, rivers, streams, lakes and ponds
seem to join at the confluence of vast super-market counters.

Checkout clerks ring up six-packs of Poland Spring,
discovering, at last, where and how to slake a mighty thirst.

SOME SMOKE-FILLED AFTERNOON

Some smoke-filled afternoon
when you are all hotness
and smoke and filled with the
urgency of green grass
and there is sunset in the air
you'll linger still and motionless
beside yourself and wonder:
wouldn't it have been better
after all, to sleep?

For as you watch that figure of a woman,
lean and delicate and presumably complete,
stir by in overbearing presumption
that even transcends the dreary heat
you'll utter silently a thought
that on the vagueness of the smoke-dream
and the hot-dust air around you,
such presumption, after all,
makes you choke.

SPRING

O spring, around the corner, you poke
your sniffling nose to see if all is clear
up ahead and whether late-bloomers
are trying to bump the line
and cut off the early-blooming crocuses
and tulips, both harbingers of your arrival.
The tulip bulbs, from Holland's shores,
have taught generations to tip-toe
and gain a foothold on the season
which brings new life.

O spring, you devil you, there is no telling
precisely when you will arrive –
though you are assigned a date.
You have dumped unexpected snow or rain, or cold,
stifled the early growth of the buds
you have in store for us -- buds that blossom
into beauty and inspire
the poets and musicians,
the lovers of all ages.

SAME OLD STORY

Unable to sleep, I get up at 3 a.m.,
twist and turn into my robe and slippers,
shuffle into the next room,
open the computer and tear off
a blank screen on the word processor,
as if it were a blank sheet of paper.
It is reminiscent of the old days
when I used paper and typewriter
to get my brain working to scribble
a few words and get the juices flowing.
It makes no difference – blank screen
or blank sheet of paper – the words
are still hard to come by.
There is no magic wand to help
construct vivid, real and coherent sentences.
They don't pop up just like that.
No electronic genie is housed in a computer,
any more than one is housed in a typewriter.
Writing is still 100 percent perspiration.
Who knows where the inspiration comes from!

THE SAND CASTLE

Sitting on the beach in a folding chair,
a hot sun beating down, I watched
the cloudless blue sky blend into the ocean's waves,
which seemed to nibble at a Winslow Homer seascape,
splashing colors onto a timeless scene,
as if my eyes had done the work of an artist's brush.

Two children, building a castle, shoveled sand
into pails and emptied them, until they had dug
a hole deep enough for a structure suitable to their tastes.
The waves edged up the beach toward the castle,
becoming stronger as the day wore on.
Soon the waves washed away much of the castle.

The children joined the waves, helping to obliterate their project,
seeming as gleeful in destroying it as they were in building it.
With their pails and shovels, the children ran off happily
into the sunset, leaving the castle in ruins,
as if they had no thoughts
of how fast it was built or how quick it was destroyed.

They left the beach under an impervious sky
and an ocean turbulent with waves --
a sign of Nature's lasting power and beauty.
And the sea, the unshakeable and strong sea,
rumbled on, reaffirming its immutability.

THE WORKSHOP

I wonder what they see in it
those lovely people who come each week
to exchange their poems and wishes
with one another and to seek

a little praise or criticism, gently given,
for the work they have done.
What they create is very personal
and criticism can touch a nerve,

so sensitive, it might do
more harm than good.
There's no guarantee what they write
will find an appreciative audience.

That's the chance they take.
They struggle in solitude to put
a few meaningful lines together.

There is always someone at the shop
willing to listen, to suggest, to amend --
not all critics think alike or are butchers.

The leader of the workshop carries the load;
he can be terse, curt, cutting you off at the pass,
even a little dictatorial,
but capable of giving good, knowledgeable words
of advise and praise, too.

That's the lay of the land --
you take it, or you had better find a new avocation.
Mostly it's fun and stimulating,
a place to find solace,
not unlike a confessional.

Be bold, get on with it,
make your words sing out, loud and clear
Who knows, you might find a spot
for your work in some anthology someday.

SNOBBERY

One of the first things to learn
when you set out to call someone a snob
is whether you have some of the same traits
you are so glib to ascribe to others.

TO THE YOUNG POETS

To the young poets, we make our plea:
the path ahead is endless.
We have had our turn and now you stand
on the podium where many a bard
has held sway.
Now you are the trumpeters.
the shapers of words and sounds and ideas,
we are eager to hear your new clarion calls.

We do not expect you to imitate or copy:
what's in a name, a rose is a rose, dancing
with the daffodils, or celebrate yourself,
or sing of yourself, or paint red wheel barrows,
or drink the milk of Paradise, or see truth
as beauty and beauty as truth, or watch
the world end, not with a bang but with a whimper,
or find the answers written in the wind,
or we are stardust, we are golden and we got
to get ourselves back to the garden.

Sing your own original songs,
make an impact, kick some butt
but remember a mule can kick back, too.
Break new ground, make no cheap bargains
and get all you are worth out of your sweat.

Viewing the World

THE CROSSING POINT

At the center stood a huge clock, on the corner stood a tavern with pretty girls and handsome beaus happily flirting and singing. I had come a long way and I was tired, but the liveliness of the girls and their beaus reinvigorated me, made me pause to remember: I, too, flirted and sang at tavern doors.

A train came through and a little boy waved at me, and an old woman, and an old man nodded at me. I thought I recognized them. When the train passed, I knew it was time to walk over the crossing point.

I began to walk across the tracks, and, as I climbed the esplanade, I looked back, and the girls and their beaus were waving at me, their kerchiefs fluttering in the air.

For a moment I thought I could go back, embrace the girls and shake hands with the beaus as I used to do. The clock rang 7 p.m.

I wanted to go back, but I didn't have the strength. So I went on. I saw a new vista in the horizon. The old vista seemed to have faded away, and everything ahead was new and shining as if it were a new world and the old world had washed away.

THE FRATERNITY

Once I was too independent
to ever think of joining a fraternity.
Such selectivity was for the elite,
not for folks brought up like me
who sometimes leaned to the left
and stood for the rights of the average person.
Fraternities were for braggarts,
hoarders, seekers after special privilege.

I had many Jewish friends
and when I was asked one day
to join a Jewish fraternity,
I gave it some thought:
Jews were liberal, caring for ideals
to better the common lot.
Jews had just gone through
a horrendous period of anti-Semitism,
Nazi persecution, holocaust, war.
What better group to stand beside?

So I joined and stood roll call
with Ordansky, Cohen, Hershkovitz, Epstein.
Goldfarb, Silberman, Saul and Stein.
Pollock, Moskowitz, Kunin and Miller,
Lister, Litsky, Levitt and Stiller.

From these seedlings blossomed
scholars, writers, editors. comedians,
athletes, lovers and scoundrels,
poker sharks, salesmen and hustlers,
doctors, lawyers and musicians.

The food was kosher, plentiful and good:
one brother ran off with the cook,

another drove his car into a brook,
a dropout couldn't stand the grind
and went off to Hollywood to rewind.

Some got tangled in the stock market,
made a fortune, then went broke;
some died young, many grew old,
some married well, some divorced,
some tried to be less Jewish,
some tried to be more Jewish.
some went to Israel to live in a Kibbutz
and some roamed 8th Avenue and the Garment District.

The brothers were witty, full of laughter,
jokes were food -- like bagels and lox --
some were sad and frugal,
others generous and happy,
but, alas, those who failed to keep
a promise were better dead.

Loud or coarse, quiet or morose,
a Jew coming of age in America
seemed to languish in an in-between purgatory,
not knowing when to hold back
or when to go full force,
traumatized, it seemed, by a society
which made him wonder
whether the world was real or unreal.

For all of this, it was plain to see:
a world without a Jew in it
would be a barren place, without spring,
a mortuary, too unreal to contemplate,
too bereft of hope, a place that simply could not be.

Who dared to say push them all into the sea?

I GENITORI — A PRAYER

The Pilgrims were the first ashore.
Then others came, struggling through .
the gates of Ellis Island, without papers,
earning the label Wops, a sobriquet
which would last a hundred years.
Guinea, Guinea Goo, why did God make you?
The Irish Micks who need not apply,
the Jewish Kikes of the Lower East Side,
the Dutch uncles and their umpah-pah-pahs,
the golden-haired Poles and their six-pack jokes,
the French frogs and a multitude of multi-national Slavs.
Many of different hues and intellectual bents
pushed their way onto the new land.
They endured the cuts and bruises,
but labored hard and prospered.
The blacks, forced to come another route,
from warmer climes and treacherous waves,
their labels embedded in skin colors
-- purple, tan, almost-white, mulatto --
that would never be eradicated,
their legs and wrists in chains.
Nobody is pure! All are warriors!
The Obamas of the world, the nannies,
the Ole Black Joes working on the levees,
toting that bale -- they took the lashes.
Oh, without them we would not have made it,
for they were the providers, the caretakers –
those who came before us -- the pathfinders.
I Genitori!
Pray for them!

GEORGE DE GREGORIO

MY BROTHER LOU

How shall I say goodbye to my brother Lou?
And how shall I remember him?
I was his kid brother, and as a boy, oh how he did love me so.

He was several years older, and I, a tangle-foot,
always wanted to go where he went,
getting in his way as he sauntered off with his pals.

He had every right to tell me to bug off;
like a shaggy dog I sniffed around, seeking a bone,
but he was too good-hearted to leave me like a stray.
So I got the best of it when he would grab my hand
and pull me along as we tried to catch up with his buddies.

How shall I say goodbye to my brother Lou?
And how shall I remember him?

I was the ammunition-bearer when he and his friends
fought the paw-paw-gun-and-mud-pie wars
with neighborhood rivals.
Our arsenal contained sandbags, rotting tomatoes,
paw-paw guns made with the inner-tubes of old tires.

Our battlefields were nearby lots and backyards
and our wounds were tomato-stained shirts.
Mom would have a fit if she knew how we got them.
"Turn the shirts inside-out, so nobody will notice them
on our way to the hamper," I told my brother.
He thought I was a genius to think of that.

We devoured the ice-box cake Mom made of graham crackers
and chocolate pudding, bananas and whipped cream;
he never learned to play drums, but he pounded away
with real sticks on a hard rubber pad in the living room

63

and imagined he was Gene Krupa.

When he went off to war, on the real battlefields,
he left me his Irish tweed coat, a beautiful garment
I wore all through high school and thought
I was Alan Ladd in "This Gun for Hire."

How shall I say goodbye to my brother Lou?
And how shall I remember him?

I was his kid brother, and as a boy, oh how he did love me so.

GEORGE DE GREGORIO

THE ANCIENT ROMANS

In all their glory, they invaded the great museum
at a cost of millions of dollars.
Sculpted in magnificent nakedness or draped
in exquisite silks in the fashion of their times.

Restored relics reliably depicting likenesses
of the great emperors of Rome -- all festooned
in hairstyles bearing strong resemblance to present-day
Caesar cuts, their physiques bulging with muscles

as if they had been groomed for the Olympics
in some high-priced Madison Avenue sports spa.
Thousands came to view these ancient relics, uninhibited
exhibitionists, their well-endowed genitalia on display.

Rarely, even in this enlightened age, has the penis
been so openly on view, idolized as it were, creating
an atmosphere of penis envy that even the gods might adore.
The hoi-poloi attended and the august *New York Times*
printed a photo of the Italian actress Gina Lollobrigitta
gazing at the relics. A floor above the main exhibition hall

stood an ancient chariot, whose ownership was in dispute
between a small town in Italy and De Montebello's
Metropolitan Museum of Art. It offered the emperors
a homegrown means of transportation in case they
were forced to make a fast getaway from New York.

.

THE POLITICIAN

From ward-heeler to governor's mansion!
a glad-handing, back-slapping impresario
wends his way among the ordinary stiffs
and with winsome boast wins their hearts.

They'll pay in taxes what he can't steal
and not one among them will call his bluff.
A little patronage here, a fruit basket there,
will go a long way to seal his re-election.

He'll fill his coffers with filthy lucre
and they'll vote him in again in a landslide.
Fund-raisers galore, studded with celebrities,
that's par for the course and worth $50 million.

That's way out of range now for common folk,
but they don't mind, they'll vote him in anyhow.
Ambition killed Caesar, and crusty Huey Long.
Bread and circuses and slot machines do the trick.

Still the pol, in all his pomp, must have his day:
his hand is out, his smile is wide and he'll wish you well.
He takes his communion with the devout electorate
like a man eating bacon and eggs at breakfast.

GEORGE DE GREGORIO

VINCENT AT THE ASYLUM

I see van Gogh alone in the asylum,
staring down a corridor,
into a courtyard filled
with a garden of greenery.

His stare is so strong
it seems as if he were trying to escape,
to leap and burst out to freedom
where he could frolic like a child.

Ever-burgeoning spring
seems to call him,
his mind and heart
yearning to be unbound.

In his mind's eye, he sees the hallway
leading to a courtyard and trees and flowers
and green brush beyond,
opening a path to eternal bliss.

That's when his brush,
clutched in the hand of genius,
takes him there, free to ramble
in the beauty of the garden.

He has transferred the view
from his imagination to the canvas,
more real and beautiful
than what he was staring at.
.

His last strokes have freed him:
he has cast out his demons,
and at 37, he has taken his own life
and cut the earthly straps that imprisoned him.

PRAISE

From the first breath, the first day, we beg for praise
as if the darkness of the womb had confined us
to an inescapable prison which bound us forever
in a place where we might never see the light.

A mother's praise we would always have in abundance,
sometimes exceeding love and overflowing to a fault.
A father's praise might have a different tint, but surely
given in love and abundance as much as a mother's

These ties, so tightly linked as if carved in stone,
we carry through the days as we seek to garner
success or failure, love or hate, victory or defeat.
It is as if we have been framed in a time capsule.

Praise is so elusive. Do we earn it merely because
we are offspring, or is it earned for something worthwhile?
It is nothing if given or won for meager or supercilious deeds.

How we accept praise is half of the equation.
In our hearts we know if it is well-deserved.
Some accept it graciously, others as if they had it coming.
Wealth, medals, high office. adulation are among the pitfalls.

Praise can lead to braggadocio and inflation of the ego,
leaving the innocence of early love behind for empty
visions of power and superiority. But stop a moment,
isn't withholding praise much worse a sin?

Maybe the poet was right, "Like trailing clouds
of glory we come from God, which is our home."
All manner of virtue or deceit are mixed in nature.
Our mission is to fulfill what is most meant for us.

GOD'S LIGHTNING BOLT

From the moment
when good citizens
went out of their minds,
so many were condemned
to death camps.

Did they not see
their fellow man
emerging,
eyes bulging,
popping out
of bony skeletons
draped
in cellophane flesh,

forever silenced,
unable to speak the unspeakable:
to tell how and why
and by whom
they had been put in such a state,

unable to utter
HATE,
invented,
like LOVE,
on the day
God
flung
the lightning bolt,
which brought forth
Adam?

Man – creature
of good and evil

greed and avarice –
builder
of civilizations,
capable
of destroying them.

A loving nature,
equally at home
with hatefulness,
warring,
peace-making,
recognizing
the power
and origin
of the flinger
of the lightning bolt.

Faithful
to him
in a fashion,
wanting
equal rights:

A standoff,
possibly forever.

"If you are God,
then I am Man."

Poetry Is Alive and Well

THE LONELY POET

O the poor lonely poet, he must be a little mad to endure the loneliness. What right has he to expect the world to genuflect at his altar?

He endures for the joy of it, the bliss of finding the right words. To him, the madness is a small price to pay to be unshackled and set free. The senseless scribbling, the frustration, seeking a soulful beginning.

He has died a thousand deaths on his journey of small victories and defeats. In the laborious search for the right colors, the tints and shadows that might create a true embrace of the human spirit, carve out the skeletal framework of a breathing, living image -- true in every aspect to the beauty of what a poem should be -- an inescapable truth he is not quite sure of.

His inventions, try as he may, are shallow and wallow in self-pity, avarice, petty lies and thievery.

And then, in his mind's eye, if he wanted to strive for more than mediocrity, there was the struggle, depending on his vantage point, to weave an ever-changing tapestry of shadows, hues, angles, boxes, circles – incalculable shapes and forms, never rigid, but always striving for beauty.

REVEILLE FOR TWO POETS

Wake up, Walt Whitman!
you've got a message:
America is still singing your songs,
you're on the Top 20 list
with the rappers and the throngs.
Lilacs still bloom in the dooryard in the spring
and the Song of Myself still holds.

Wake up, William Carlos Williams!
a telegram for you, sir.
Paterson is alive and teeming
as Latinos and blacks and others
yearn to breathe free.
Your Catholic Bells are still ringing
and the Red Wheel Barrow
is still catching rain water.
Your little old sleepy hometown
has broken out the glad-rags and celebrated your 125th
with a symposium of your songs -- ad infinitum.

Don't laugh Walt! Don't laugh Carlos!
Your poetic clout still keeps America singing.
Together, you bridged three centuries
to this historic moment:
Obama, a black man,
and Hillary, a woman, together
are the first of their kind
to trade gibes in pursuit of a nomination
for President of the United States.

In the bank the other day
your songs were on full display.

The young teller was a beautiful Thai girl.
Her nameplate told it all:
she had become Mrs. Harrington, USA.

Get the pitch, Walt? What do you say, Carlos?
America is still singing your triumphant songs.
Your songs of prophecy have lasted longer
than you had hoped.

Your songs have spawned an epidemic
which has infected 300 million;
there's no telling what changes they will bring:
a calm or a whirlwind.

WHEN YOU ARE IN THE WAY

When you are in the way, excuse yourself.
don't let the lady sense you are a clod or a bore.
She may have something to offer
and you might get lucky and find a partner.

Much has accrued to gentlemanly manners,
even in the most precarious times.
It is better to disappear than to stumble
and upset the serving cart or to bump

the poor waiter and fall into a lady's lap,
though, all pretense aside, that would be
a most delightful way to resolve
your predicament and end it on a happy note.

THANKSGIVING DAY — 2006

Karen drove us from New Jersey
to Pennsylvania, past the naked trees
that had shed their leaves
along the highway, telltale signs
of one season ending,
making way for the next.
It had been a pleasant day, a big dinner
cooked by her uncle, good wine,
all the trimmings, even a few jokes
(not everyone laughed).
Karen checked her messages:
Laurie had called to say
her mother had just passed away.
Karen's voice quivered on the phone.
She had worked with the mother,
a French lady who taught that language,
and loved all kinds of poetry.
Lung cancer took her at 68,
Laurie had given birth to Jacques
two years earlier, only days
before the doctors confirmed
that the mother's cancer was terminal.
Karen visited the mother at hospital
a day after she had come out of a coma.
They talked about teaching, family, a trip
to Paris, and about little Jacques.
Nature has its way of replenishing itself.

THE CELL PHONE

Are you one of those polluters of air
who must carry a cell phone everywhere?
Do you crank it out in a supermarket
while waiting for your order to be checked out?

How about at the movies, or in a taxi, or in your car?
Or waiting at the curb for a bus, or in the bus?
Do you stick it under your pillow at night just in case
your husband's or your wife's entreaties are too disarming?

Perhaps you've got it cleverly concealed in church
so, if need be, you can communicate miles away
with your daughter, or a friend, to make a date
to meet at the hairdresser's or just anywhere.

Do you ever stop to think you are breaking a silence
and invading someone else's privacy or peace
of mind, let alone an atmosphere of quiet dignity?
I guess embarrassment doesn't occur to you.

It's understandable how practical and useful
a cell phone can be in the dark of night
when your car is on the fritz and you are marooned
miles from home without a friend in sight.

Conceded, it's big in business and for closing deals,
but cell phone users go on for hours: Often their conversation
seems inane and trivial. "I'll be home in 10 minutes,
I'm only a few blocks away." "Please check my mail."
"Look up Sarah's number for me." "I've had a rough day."

Cell phones have become universal pests from China to Timbuktu.
They number in the billions and are multiplying faster
than rodents. We're overrun and there's no turning back.
Progress? We're getting an earful! Somebody, please, hang up!

THE COFFEE SHOP

Stopping early at the coffee shop in town:
to some it's a rite of passage, a place to meet,
a face-to-face challenge with neighbors and reality,
striving to remake the world in our own image.

Millions of folks succumb to the same folly,
but it's a nice way to start the day, a pepper-upper
that gets your juices flowing and your head
stuck on the right way to face what's coming.

Take Pop, an octogenarian, who angrily lashes out
at the current Administration no matter the party,
calling for the repeal of tax laws, gun control,
abortion and whatever else defiles the landscape.

It's a place for the opinionated to vent their fury
and often it takes on the ferocity of a mini-storm.
In the end even the most heated tend to back off,
hoping to fight another day, same place same cast.

In some, there lurks a stubborn streak that tends
to take away the fun of it all and makes you wish
there could be an arbiter softening and settling
the outbursts of prejudice and down-right hatred.

Minds get twisted and misunderstandings reign.
A friendly argument can lose all perspective and reason.
I love the coffee shop, but I hope some day
it will snuff out ugliness and revive
the common sense kindred spirits have for one another.

THE FRENCH HAVE THE WORD FOR IT

In all the languages at man's disposal,
merde might be the most delicate word
when it comes to describing itself,
thus acquiring, as the French might say,
a universal acceptance and appeal.
So, to all those who would change the world,
I say you are full of *merde*,
and will be full of it when you are gone.

You might change the world
when the world wants to change,
when it wants to cast greed and hate into the sea
and clean up its act.
Until then, the waiters of haute cuisine,
the fawners over wallets filled with greenbacks,
will maintain their status as servile clowns.

Their crap is so full-blown and windswept
it travels from continent to continent
polluting everything it touches.
They belittle the teary-eyed child
in her innocence and tell her lies,
preach to the bedraggled working man,
and even those who achieve riches and fame,
that they possess the magic wand
to wave away the sins of the world.

They are truly full of it,
so full of it, they cannot see it
rising like the tide
to cover their eyes
and blind them
and drown them,
as the French might say,
in *une mer de merde.*

TITILLATION

The women come and go,
talking of "The DaVinci Code"
while on a shopping spree at the mall.
Cell phones on the ladies' ears, sound
their own cacophony,
as tight pants and skirts above the knees,
bosoms hanging long and loose,
not for feeding (though that exists, too)
but for titillation and lifting eyebrows
of men and women and children.
Are they false or real?
Does it matter?

The effect is the same and someday
credit cards will be no more.
Identities will be gone, stolen, dissolved.
and the world might listen then
to the birds and the trill and the chirp
of the nightingales and there will be
no pigons on the avenue to defile landmarks,
nor proud eagles molting and building nests
atop the swank facades on Fifth Avenue.

The world will have come to a stop
and we'll all get off.
Then it will start spinning again,
round and round and round and round...

NEVER GIVE UP

I asked a friend to read my poetry
for he was known to have an ear
that could discern the good from the bad
and if he heard music he would tell you
and if he heard sour notes he would tell you.

He was an honest critic. and would not lead you astray.
His range was broad, from Kubla Khan to Dover Beach,
from Prufrock to Red Wheel Barrows.
His work was hard and harder still
when asked to appraise the jottings of a friend.

That is the hardest task of all – to tell a friend
his poetry is not quite up to snuff, or being generous
to say "it's just a tad off the mark."
How do you let him down gently,
without hurting his feelings, without wounding
his ego, without discouraging him from future efforts?

Being diplomatic, my friend might say:
"Keep on writing, keep coming back,"
or, true to himself, he might use the Churchillian plea:
"Never give up, never, never give up."

THE COMPUTER

They say it's an indispensable machine,
it'll solve so many mundane problems
and emancipate you from drudgery
and introduce you to skullduggery.

Almost everyone from 6 to 96
is acquainted with the mouse and the icon
but some are so erudite they can become
millionaires overnight -- in the stock market.

I am still among the army of resisters
who pooh-poohs its intellectual pluses
and still takes lessons from his sisters
keeping his fingers from getting blisters.

You can buy one rather cheaply now
and starting with a reference book for dummies
attain a modicum of utility to keep you abreast
with the latest water-cooler office pests.

If you can avoid the snobbery of those so good
at formulating fancy formats, you'll achieve
an independence so special you can tell
them all to go fly a kite or go to Hell!

But that is gauche and shows a hard-headedness
toward progress. The computer, after all, drives
the economy, the social scene and education.
Isn't it the force behind the GDP and procreation?.

So let us not make light of this giant of an invention.
Like money and cars, television and radio, it's here to stay.
It can entertain and teach, with a broad reach.
On dreary days, it can offer mischief, or keep us out of trouble!

KILLING TREES

The majestic maples, elms and oaks
that lined our neighbor's property
were like old friends, friendlier
even than the grouchy neighbor
who posted No Trespassing signs
on the grounds. Their size testified
to their grandeur, big and leafy
and 50 or even 100 years old.
Children leaped and played beneath
their branches.

In his small world, our neighbor
saw the trees standing in the way,
impediments to his capitalizing on the land.
Workmen came with saws
and trucks and "cut 'em all down."
It was like a blitzkrieg.
When the buzz saws stopped
there was a loud silence.
"Good job," our neighbor said, as he paid the workers.
To the hired hands, killing trees, was simply a way
of making a living – no remorse, no emotion.

A Talmudic verse reminds us: "I did not find
the world desolate when I entered it
and as my fathers planted for me
so do I plant for my children."

LET THE WORDS BLEED

Writing poems is hard, lonely work,
like this one, started yesterday.
You don't know where it's going.
and you must be mad to start it
in the first place and think some reader
will genuflect at your desktop..
Conceited, daring?

But why not? In this business
they tell you to find your inner need,
let it all out, empty your head
of all the cobweb-like, dusty stuff
you've been storing in there,
making you confused and screwed up,
sucking the guts out of your inner self –

the part of you that longs to be set free,
to expiate your soul and give you
the grace to kneel in prayer
to the Almighty and thank Him
for the sublime you in you.

Maybe a melodic chord will emerge
or a nerve will be hit and produce
a great speech or line.
Women might be a pursuit
more exciting and rewarding,
but they can give you trouble, too.

You seek exciting images you can hook your hat on
or offer food you can sink your teeth into.
Most of all, words shouldn't
be so limp that they forget

what they are meant to say.
If they were intended to be funny,
let them be full-blown-funny,
not half-ass funny, or half-ass true
or half-ass beautiful.
Go all the way, scratch their asses,
let the bastard words bleed.

JOY

What is joy?

Joy is rapture,
enthralling,
full of promise,
void of exploitation,
simple.

You cannot reach it
by negotiation.

IF ONLY I COULD WRITE A POEM

If only I could write a poem
straightforward, honest, no frills,

leaving out the egocentric
self-serving, confusing words

which always get in the way.
If only once I could scribble

a confession, a contrition,
restore my soul, egoless,

to the purity of my childhood,
be engaged with the sinew

of a child's limbs reaching out
in the sexual embrace of new life,

free, unencumbered, like the acorn
that might become a tree,

spawning, multiplying,
existing for its own sake,

like in a primeval forest.
If only once I could write a poem

from the heart,

I would be thankful and feel
I had paid my debt in full.

GEORGE DE GREGORIO

HOW DO YOU LIKE YOUR EGGS?

Home is where they ask you,
"How do you like your eggs?"
And you say, "Ah, screw it.
I'll just have a hamburger."

Aren't we all a little betwixt and between,
unable to decide right off the bat
what we like or where we want to be?

We have no idea
how long the journey will be,
so we hem and haw, vacillate
like little children trying to decide

whether our favorite flavor
is grape or orange or lemon-lime.
God forbid we should grow up so fast,
knowing what we like and don't like,

where we are headed and driving
at full speed along an endless highway.
We are in the vortex, looking
for ways to get out, looking

for a full life, a little bit of everything,
a smorgasbord, so full and brimming
with the force of inhaling and exhaling
you feel you are going to burst
from the love that is piling up inside.

What would you give for this cornucopia,
this drunkenness of life?

HOW TO EARN A BRAVO

A bravo is not easily earned.
Its origin is not exactly known.
Some crazy Italian must have let his hair down
after a rousing aria, and shouted:
"Bravo! Bravo!"
not knowing what the consequences would be.

Grand opera seems to have given it birth,
and weaned a very prejudiced concept.
Critics rarely offer it and rarely get one themselves.
Simplicity or sophistication are the barometers,
but excellence is the currency.

Who is to say which genius or pedestrian
deserves a bravo, and for what?
A comic, for laughter?
A vagabond, for idleness?
A chef?
A lover?
The trick is to hold it back,
not giving a bravo to just anyone,
for just a trifling accomplishment.

FRIENDSHIP

Making friends is a delicate business.
You say, he or she is my best friend,
choosing from a lifetime of acquaintances,
someone you hope you can trust.

Making friends, after all, is more pursuit
than necessity, although friends are good
for social well-being and grace.
Friends show many faces of loyalty and sincerity.

Most pay allegiance first to family ties and deem
a mere "friend" as an intruder, bent on breaking
strong bonds that are sometimes taken for granted,
leaving little room for curiosity and growth.

Growing up, you may have a strong attachment,
but it is not easy to latch onto a lasting pal.
That a man lay down his life for his friend
is still among the great virtues.

But who among us can rise to such sacrifice?

BUTTERFLIES

Breaking through the serpentine walls
of its cocoon, full-blown,
emerging as if from nowhere,
flying overhead at the bus stop,
circling as if to engage you in conversation:
"Look! I am free!
I ascend of my own free will.
I fly! I am king of all I survey."
What a destiny! If only briefly.

You have yet to fulfill your own destiny.
For now, you know the bus will take you
deep into the city's concrete cocoon
and you will swelter in the 94-degree heat
or freeze in the 12-inch blizzard.
But what about the rest of the time?

The butterfly still circles above you,
still trying to communicate.
Its freedom is so liberating, it makes you feel
imprisoned by your job and family ties.
No matter where you go, you are caught.
Jail cells are not the only prisons.
You board the bus for the city,
 leaving your new friend and wondering
why you were picked to think about the future.

If butterflies are free, then why not me?

BREAKFAST

*(An imitation of W.C. Williams'
"This Is Just to Say"}*

The green, inedible banana
lay cut in half
in the basket.

"You cut the banana,"
she said, snappishly.

"Yes, I made a mistake,"
I said.

"I had put out the canned
peaches," she said..

"I know," I said.

And then I drank the rest of my cup
of coffee.

AUTUMN DOODLING

Sweet is the night air
when summer empties into fall
and awakens the brain and heart
to a new rapture, so sublime,
the drug-like feeling,
bathed in bliss, never ends.

The awakening doesn't take much:
the simple act of changing the clock,
of spending time in a small café,
arouses the senses and gives
the night a new glow.

You are repositioned for acceptance,
anticipation, arousal, pleasure.
It happens again and again
-- despite all calamities –
as the seasons complete
their inevitable cycle.

We are awed by the magic,
the certainty that Nature
has made her rounds,
and, all else failing.
has kept her promises.

AT YEAR'S END

Time to take stock,
pick a new shaving cream
take the change in the cigar box
to the shopping center
and cash in.
Holidays come pretty fast,
you'll need all the cash
you can get just to stay even.
The whole year compressed
into a few days, a week.
At year's end, we may settle
for a toast at midnight, or a kiss,
or a good-luck wish whispered
to those we love.

A TINCTURE OF TIME

Afternoon cappuccino, unlike afternoon tea,
brimmed their cups with foamy, sudsy hot milk.

The ladies talked and drank away the afternoon,.
seeing little they thought worth taking with them.

They frittered time away -- a tincture of time,
a threshold, a window that doctors called

a healer when no other diagnosis existed
and they waited until the tincture kicked in

and helped heal all wounds and maladies.
Medical men are superstitious, too.

The ladies rose and left, not noticing
where time went or how much of it

they had spent or how valuable it was
when it was so sorely needed.

AT A SAFE DISTANCE

Her long legs, exuding strength, stride along
the exit ramp from the Nieman-Marcus store.
Her gait is deliberate, practiced, as if she were schooled
to get the most out of her stature. It could be a capital gain.

She has other lovely attributes, easily noticeable
and voluptuous: a lovely face, curvaceous body.
A valet-parking attendant goes for her car, leaving her
to stand by, deftly handling the packages she is carrying.

A man in a car nearby has been watching her
since she first stepped out of the store.
He admires her beauty as his elbow inadvertently
presses the horn, touching off a shrill cacophony.

He turns off the ignition; embarrassed, he wishes he could
find a hole to hide in as the woman sends a smile his way.
The valet returns with the car and she gets in with aplomb,
never losing a beat, and quietly drives away.

THE FINAL CURTAIN

Not having experienced it, death is something
I'd rather skip. Jesus gave Lazarus a second chance,
but he didn't stay around long enough
for an interview to tell us what happened.

A lot of folks, when they are depressed, say:
"I wish I were dead." They don't really mean it.
What they really mean is: wouldn't it be great to go
where Lazarus went and get back in time for dinner.

People say, "Drop dead!" to friend and foe alike,
usually when they are hot under the collar.
You hear, "Death where is thy sting?" --
words usually heard from the pulpit or in a hymn

or at a funeral for a real stiff who can't answer
and tell us how painful and permanent the sting really is.
There are a lot of silly bromides about death:
"I'll be glad when you're dead you rascal you"

and "Till death do us part" implying a superficial
joy and a long-lasting dubious loyalty.
Death comes on the battlefield, in a car or plane crash,
by murder, tsunami, lethal injection, illness, suicide.
A zillion different ways. No cards can trump it.

Someday we'll all catch up with it.
The thing is to have fun while the longevity lasts.
What the hey, we can't live forever!
Meanwhile tell yourself:
"Living long and well is the best revenge."

REMEMBERING
(A prose poem)

"Your father was a frustrated man,"
my mother said to me on one of my visits,
sitting in her room, barely able to see.
She waved her thin, feeble, bony-looking
hands, beckoning me to come closer
so she could hold my hands in hers.
"He wanted so much to make a go of it,
but he just never got the chance."
"I know Mom," I said."I know he tried."

It was a peaceful visit, all rancor gone,
no time for recriminations.
It was time to sublimate our feelings,
go deep down into our inner selves
to make a contrition worthy of mother
and son to find forgiveness -- as if we
were making a confession to each other,
filled with loving memories of all that went before.
"Pop was a good man," I said, generous
in my appraisal, knowing full well
that they had had skirmishes and battle
royales in their younger days, especially
bringing up three sons. That's how the visit went.

I visited as often as I could since I lived out of town.
The last visit would always stay with me.
Mom, who had been a heavy-set, buxom woman,
had scaled down to about 100 pounds,
and was confined to bed most of the day.
She lived in the same house, actually her house,
with my older brother and his wife.
She was in bed when I arrived
and had been refusing nourishment --

a bite here, a bite there -- for several weeks
"Why am I here?" she would ask.
"Why doesn't the Eternal Father take me?"

She had a sweet-tooth to rival the most
avid sweets aficionado anywhere – ice cream
was her favorite and Italian pastries
and cookies -- canoli, esfogliatelli, rum cakes,
"How about some ice cream?" I asked her.
She agreed and I spooned a few mouthfuls
which she took feebly, half-heartedly,
obviously with little appetite.
I sat beside her on the bed and we held hands.
She clutched my hands strongly,
the way she did on my previous visit,
and we remained that way, it seemed,
for the longest time, not saying a word.

I learned later that my brother and his wife
were going to put her in a nursing home.
They had lived with her for 25 years
and it must have been a shock to my mother
to learn that they planned to take her out
of her home. A couple of days after my last visit,
I received a phone call. Mom had passed away at home.
Her refusal to eat must have been her strategy
to starve herself so she could die in her own bed.
It was the last week in January and snow
was on the ground. In March, she would have
celebrated her 103rd birthday.

The Winds of War

D-DAY 61 YEARS LATER

I remember when my brother returned home, moody, sullen, embittered. He had seen combat but he wouldn't talk about it. He kept it pent up, gnawing at him, too proud to let it all out. It took "Saving Private Ryan" and Parkinson's and one of my phone calls to the nursing home to finally extract the pride and honor he felt about being there in France with his buddies. "Today is D-Day, 61 years ago," I said. "All that time," he said, Parkinson's impeding his speech. "Hard to believe I didn't talk about it much," he said, "but we had a good bunch, a lot of fellows from our town." Sixty of his buddies were detached from his unit to make the first landing on Omaha Beach. "Come with us Lou, we got plenty of room," they laughed and shouted in guarded anticipation. For a while he thought about whether to follow. "They're a bunch of fuck-ups, Lou," he heard his first sergeant say. "You stick by your orders."

The next day, he and the rest of his unit made the landing. Just as it was depicted in "Saving Private Ryan," the beach was clear and smooth after the hellish carnage. As they went ashore, a voice called out, "Hey Lou, it's all right, they've been driven inland." He had never felt such surprise and consternation. One of his buddies had spotted him and gave him the all clear. Machine gun fire rattled around the men, shell holes dotted the beach. Some of the soldiers skirted around them, others saw they would make good safe foxholes. Only five men from his unit didn't make it back. "We used to have a reunion in New York for a few years, and the fellow who called out my name on the beach called me once, but as the years went by we sort of lost touch."

100

He was not a hero and he was grateful that he wasn't hurt. He refused a promotion to corporal on the field but he never said why he refused it. The strain of more than three years in the war never really seemed to go away. He got married and they had a son. And 61 years later his beach was a tiny room in a nursing home out in the countryside where his wife and son had decided he needed to be because of his Parkinson's Disease. The doctor called it the beginning stages of the illness, but his incontinence and a fall one day, after he was sent home from the nursing home, betrayed his lack of improvement and set up the relapse. It was too much for his wife to handle, she said, even with a visiting nurse and help coming in. She was ill, too, and not used to having people around interfering with her routine. So my brother went back to the cubbyhole. After five years in the nursing home and a 10-year battle with Parkinson's, my brother, Lou, died quietly on June 29, 2009. A nurse from the staff hugged him close and told my nephew she loved his father. A couple of months before, his wife, frail and weak from a battery of illnesses, was admitted to the same nursing home. She was still there when Lou died, and was too ill to attend his funeral.

NO CURE, NO PEACE

An advertisement breaks
into the morning radio talk show,
and says it has the panacea,
God's solution to your pain.
The advertiser is legitimate,
the NYU Health Center.
It can help cure arthritis,
spinal stenosis, osteoporosis, neuropathy,
shingles, diabetes, piss and bliss,
almost anything that might restore
the spine to a normal state
and get you standing straight.

But what about Fallujah?

You see a new life ahead,
the cane swallowed by the wind,
a trip to Europe -- Italy, Paris, Spain --
who knows, maybe even Machu Picchu.
You recite your ailments,
the list is very long.
You want to straighten up,
go window shopping,
send the bent-over stoop
into oblivion.

But what about the treacherous
streets of Baghdad?

No more dragging ass
like an old fart, who has grown invisible.
You sense sympathy from the lady
on the phone – maybe you don't sound so old to her.
"Is the procedure noninvasive?"

"No, it's like a regular operation."
"You mean you rehab for 6 months?"
"That's about it."
"Then why the big promo on radio?"

And what about the wounded
and the paraplegics at Walter Reed?

Why are you listening
to the fucking radio anyway?
It's just one more con
the world is putting over on you.
There's no cure-all, there never was.
You'll take back the pain,
go back to the cane,
your old trusted friend.

But what about the dead and maimed
strewn on the desert plains,
the youthful seedlings that might
have blossomed into flowers?

SOLDIER'S SONG

*(Written as a tribute to Sean Patrick Fennerty, who died in Iraq
at the age of 23 in 2007 in a roadside bombing)*

*Oh, sweet Jesus, stay with me,
I am off to war and will need your shield.*

Though the Iraq desert engulfs me now
the Oregon sky will forever shine on me.

*Oh, sweet Jesus, stay with me,
I am off to war and will need your shield.*

Sean Patrick you are going off to danger,
his mother, Mo, and his father, Brian, said.

You will be brave and do your duty,
you always wanted to do your part.

That's what they taught you at school,
and you always had that in your heart.

*Oh. sweet Jesus, stay with me,
I am off to war and will need your shield.*

In the hotness of the day, a bomb went off
and struck your heart and killed you on the roadside.

He's too young to die, his mother wept,
his father turned to his other children

and weeping they all knelt in prayer,
saying the orison they knew Sean knew so well

Oh, sweet Jesus, stay with me,

GEORGE DE GREGORIO

I am off to war and will need your shield.

He skied on the hills and fished in the waters
all over the glorious big sky country.

He loved his friends and his family
and always said he wanted to be a soldier,

to serve his country and to spread the word
of freedom's song, his soldier's song.

Oh, sweet Jesus, stay with me,
I am off to war and will need your shield.

TERROR

The thought of terror makes mothers cringe.
They are the first to feel the threat and know
intuitively what dangers lurk, for their concern,
while others frolic, is safety for their children.

They envision the possible dark confrontation
as if it were one more duty in the multi-daily
chores of raising their broods. They handle it
like soldiers training and preparing for battle.

There is no fooling mothers when it comes to terror.
They will scratch and claw for self-preservation
and preservation of their families, in the face
of suicidal bombings and other acts of murderous evil.

They are like the lioness who senses encroachment
and knows that she alone stands between her young
and the intruders seeking to invade her habitat.
The jungle is not unlike the dwelling of modern man.

This terror that makes daily life so tenuous and shaky,
spills a kind of venom over the land and almost makes
humanity lose its humanness, casting fear that paralyzes
even the best of us into skeptical non-involvement.

Mothers are involved by Nature; those who stand aside.
for whatever reasons, do not realize the fitful costs
hesitancy and non-commitment have in store for them.
Terrorists have broken down the laws of human decency.

If we can stand alongside the lioness to protect our young,
there may still be a chance for humankind to express:
courage, strength, faith and a will to endure.

THE LITTLE PRIEST

Recruited early, a small, slim, unobtrusive man,
a good candidate for obedience and loyalty,
he took the vows without regret or remorse
and went happily to the altar with an open heart.
Roving eyes caught the splendor of young girls
passing in summer skirts on hot city sidewalks.
Fire fighters, brawny, brave and strong,
hearing the wailing alarms, had chosen him as chaplain.
Ordained as a youth, imbued with the fire,
straying from orthodoxy, seeking fortune in men's eyes,
sinking into stupors and digging himself out,
reaching for courage and burning to embrace truth.
On a fateful Tuesday morning,
the sun so exhilaratingly aflame
that Dante's inferno seemed to convulse into life
and consumed the Twin Towers,
the little priest, as he gave communion,
felt burning steel and fire collapse around him
and surrendered to the Great Intruder.
Amid the carnage, fire fighters,
draped their arms around the body
and carried it to a nearby church,
where, at last, the little priest found a place to rest.

PUTNAM, CONNECTICUT

So far away from Ground Zero,
this little town of 9,000,
once teeming with mills,
but now a center for antiques,
pasted its silent tributes
on the three-mile fence
along the winding walking path.
Its hearts and souls
as wounded as the big city.

BROTHERS

I am lucky to have two older brothers.
They were drafted and went to the big war.
After the war, I enlisted and went to Japan.
Both of my brothers went to Europe to fight.

None of us was a hero and I was glad
we all came home alive and grew old.
I remember the day the war in Europe ended.
I was a senior in high school in Mr. Burton's class.
.

I guess I was so filled with emotion that day
that Mr. Burton said: "Why are you crying son?"
I said I had two brothers in the Army in Europe
and that they'd be coming home safe and sound.

"Oh, that's wonderful," Mr. Burton said. "I know
how happy you and your family must feel."
It took awhile for my brothers to come home:
the Army didn't discharge them just like that.

In fact, my brothers were going to be rotated,
which meant they would have to train to go fight the Japanese.
I guess fighting the Nazis for three years wasn't enough.
Anyway, I was a camp counselor when the A-Bomb fell.

One of my brothers was on furlough
and he came to camp to see me.
We hugged for ten minutes and we cried we were so happy.
Even the old chef at the camp and my cousin,
who drove my brother to see me, had watery eyes that day.

My other brother came home, too, and my mother
and father were happy and we celebrated.
The war had taken a good chunk out of many lives
and some would never know what a difference it made.

ARMISTICE DAY

By early afternoon,
the parade was over,
we walked home
with flags and balloons.
Sousa marches echoed in our ears
and thoughts turned
to food and baseball.
The guns of World War I
had not been silent very long.
Now, distant rumbles
were heard again

Old soldiers, in frayed uniforms,
gathered in the street,
limping toward the small shingled houses.
Veterans, making their annual foray,
were seeking handouts
in the poor working-class neighborhood
where they felt welcome
and comfortable and knew
they would not be turned away.

One held a tin cup, another hobbled on a crutch,
another, legless, maneuvered his torso on a gurney.
Through a megaphone, a coarse voice warbled:
"My buddy, my buddy, your buddy misses you."
They had fought in the "war to end all wars."

Hitler and Mussolini
rubbed each other's backs.
Poland fell like whipped cream
and the London blitz raised the backs
of a proud and courageous people
while Hirohito, asleep at his castle,

enabled Pearl Harbor.

It was the same old story:
"a fight for love and glory."
Those who had not died,
as always, straggled
home to heal their wounds
and repair their hearts and minds
to try again to fit into a reasonable life.

MEMORIAL DAY 2009

"Get there if you can and see the land you once were proud to
  own
though the roads have almost vanished and the expresses never
  run: . . . .
If you really want to live, you'd better start at once to try,
if you don't, it doesn't matter, but you better start to die."

from W. H. Auden's "Get There If You Can," 1945

The bomb is on its way, the bomb is one its way.
Build your rat holes, build your shelters.
Kim Jong Il has his sights set on whoever bats an eye.
All are targeted for destruction, getting-even time is near.

The Earth is rumbling, a thunderous din tests the sky.
While Koreans are foraging for food,
Kim has a new toy to play catch-up with.
Hiroshima and Nagasaki were nothing
compared to what he has in store.

Memory, old memory, do not let us down,
exhume the ingrained thoughts we cannot forget.
Who will speak out? Remember 1939, 1941, 1944, 1945,
Poland, Pearl Harbor, D-Day, V-J Day on the Missouri.

Japanese cities flattened to a crisp, reduced to rubble;
men, women and children incinerated,
erased, as if they had never existed,
What can their census-takers matter now?

Kim's bomb is as powerful as the one dropped on Hiroshima.
The leader has been practicing a lot lately,
and he is nuts about gadgets, things that go poof in the night,
and music that spins a yarn and keeps his hips rotating.

GEORGE DE GREGORIO

Memory, old memory do not let us down.
The soldiers are passing by, the living and the dead;
decorate their graves with flags and flowers. Their job is done.
Life is a gift and we have trampled upon it.

If Kim gets his way. the roads of New York, Boston,
Los Angeles, Detroit, and many big and little byways,
will have vanished and the expresses will never run.
We only ask that when we die,
they bury us where God is standing by!

A TOAST TO LONDON TOWN

I have never been to London Town
(except for a short layover at Heathrow).
I have never seen Judy Garland at the Palladium,
but I have been to Yankee Stadium.

Although I strive to be a poet
I have never been to Poets' Corner
at Westminster where the famous are buried.
I have never gazed at the stones that cover
Tennyson, Coleridge and Wordsworth,
a triumvirate worthy of a wager on a Trifecta.
I have never been to an English pub to sing,
(until I turned blue in the cheeks)

"I've got a lovely bunch of coconuts."

I have never been to the Music Hall
where the roguish Archie Rices
of the world used to strut their stuff.
I have never seen the changing of the guard
(in person, that is) at the Palace
or taken a cab to Trafalgar Square.
or made a speech in Hyde Park
or stood with the survivors of the blitz and sung

*"There'll be blue birds over the white cliffs of Dover,
tomorrow when the world is free."*

THE ALLIGATOR SUITCASE

A cheap cardboard suitcase purchased
at the PX in Japan before I left for stateside.
It went with me everywhere, a tagalong,
like a little brother I couldn't shake off.

Eventually, it served as a collector of scraps
of writings I hoped someday to turn into a great novel.
It went with me the summer I spent in Montana
cutting trails and working as a lookout,
scribbling and filling notebooks with youthful thoughts.

Alas, I let it down. And lingering there,
collecting dust, and turning yellow are clippings
of old newspaper accounts of stories I wrote
in my early days – some even promising.

I call it my alligator suitcase because the designers
of such cheap merchandise made the exterior look
like alligator skin -- a feature in those days
mostly for expensive stuff and copied by vendors
of really cheap materials -- they do that a lot these days , too.

My Japanese souvenirs are images of little kids
and little old ladies foraging in garbage cans
for something to eat amid a surrounding
beauty of cherry blossoms and wild sunflowers
.

The suitcase harbored many memories and notes,
even a love letter or two, and evaluations of life
which a young man thinks will cure
the world's illnesses and inequities.

It loomed now in the dusty, drafty attic
where dreams are stored. It finally made it downstairs

into our home again, where we sat round as if discovering
a lost artifact of some bygone age, a slice of life
suppressed for so long by everyday, hard-working,
humdrum chores too mundane to overcome.

The suitcase is like a natural appendage now
and will stay downstairs until the time comes
for somebody to inspect and discard or save
its contents, maybe even try to make heads or tails
about what is in it and why it was kept for so long.

An old suitcase, brimming with young and old ideas,
resting there, hoping the spirit will breathe new life
into it and save it from the eternal ashcan of oblivion.

Oh, for a chance again to face new challenges ahead,
alligator suitcase in hand, heading out, hoping
to find a new burst of cherry blossoms
and wild sunflowers in the spring.

The Sporting Life

WE ALMOST WON

Ten o'clock on a Sunday morning most folks are in church unless, of course, they're getting ready to play in the Sunday Morning Softball League: a ritual as important as going to prayer services.

In our town no roosters crowed to get us up, we were roused by Grandpa or the alarm clock. You gave up the extra sleep on Sunday morning so you could play ball, envisioning your stardom.

You were 10 years old and you looked up to your older brothers and the other guys on the team. You kept the scorecard, you knew the lineup, you lived and died with every pitch, hit or out.

The players liked to have fun and laughed and clowned while shagging fly balls and playing pepper, waiting for the game to start. You saw an ominous sign in their light-hearted attitude about the game.

They played hard enough and scruffed your head after a good play and you jotted everything down. The score might swell to a five-run lead in the fifth inning, good enough, you thought, to go home a winner this time.

By the seventh, the lead had vanished and the team once again was on the losing end. That made you angry. You had detected the tragic flaw -- the clowning and laughing. In the car on the way home you cried, "You guys stink!"

Everybody laughed and they admitted how badly they played. "We only made three errors," they laughed. "We almost won." Your 10-year-old heart would have none of that. "You lost because you didn't care about winning."

A few years later, a Sunday morning was reserved for the attack on Pearl Harbor, and all the boys of that softball team went off to war and nothing was quite the same again.

IT IS PRETTY HARD TO TAKE

It is pretty hard to take,
after all these years,
when they tell me the game
is rigged and Clemens
and A-Rod and Bonds
and several others
have used steroids
and human growth hormones
to extend their baseball lives.

It is pretty hard to take,
especially when you consider
the millions of dollars
these fellows are paid
to frolic on the ball field
just passing the time of day;
They even throw in two months
to train in warm-weather climes.

It is pretty hard to take,
especially when I read
and watch the news about the kids
starving in Africa who could
use some of that H.G.H. stuff to help
eradicate diseases that are
killing them left and right.
Our priorities just aren't right.

It is pretty hard to take,
especially when the records
of Ruth and Aaron and Maris are replaced
with asterisks to explain why
the new record is tainted
and baseball has to make excuses

to put it in the good book.

It is pretty hard to take,
after all these years, just about
when I am ready to check out,
that the game all us kids played
in dusty sandlots is so slick now
that there's no room left to dream
we could all be like Roy Hobbs
and just play the game for the love of it.

MR. GEHRIG MEET MR. JETER

Somehow, wherever it is that old ballplayers
spend their time after their days on Earth –
having a beer or a cup of coffee in a place
something like a locker room or a dugout --
somehow they always get the news
about what is happening down below.
Don't fool yourself, ballplayers know everything
about what is going on in baseball all the time.

So it is likely that Mr. Gehrig got the news,
wherever he is, that Mr. Jeter had moved ahead of him
on the Yankees' all-time list for most hits,
just as he had received the news that Cal Ripken
had passed his consecutive-games playing streak.
Mr. Gehrig lost those records and he got an even tougher break
when illness paralyzed him and he died much too young.

Lou Gehrig and Derek Jeter seem to have been made
of the same cloth – quiet, gentle souls, brought up
straight – maybe you could say Mamma's boys –
but possessed of a work ethic that transcended
everything when it comes to playing the game.
That's what the players call baseball – the game.
Babe Ruth, in his dying days, said baseball
"is the greatest game -- the only game."

All records are made to be broken and pass
from generation to generation, just as it says
in the Good Book – the sun also rises.
Mr. Gehrig is fortunate because good men
have surpassed his marks, and there is no taint
associated with them unlike the records of The Babe
whose marks have been clouded by the intrusion
of substances that enhanced the power of the record-breakers.

Not Maris or Aaron, of course, but other interlopers.

Mr. Jeter is a gentleman who will likely go on
to establish more records and extend the one
which Mr. Gehrig worked so hard ro make.
Mr. Gehrig said: "I consider myself the luckiest man
on the face of the Earth," when he bowed out
from baseball and public view. Who's to say he was not?
The time may come when Mr. Jeter may say the same thing.

Old ballplayers, like old soldiers, never die, they just fade away.

THAT DAY IN ARIZONA (Super Bowl, 2008)

The haughty Patriots, unbeaten in 18 games,
stood tall near the gates of Valhalla.
Eli swerved, Eli eluded, Eli kept his cool,
Eli escaped all harm from the clutches
of a swarm of ferocious behemoths,
his jersey fluttering behind him
while 100 million kept their eyes upon him.

That day in Arizona,
the Giants were full of fight.

They blitzed and sacked
like Roman legions pillaging a helpless town.
The Giants were young and old,
eleven rookies in all, as they sent
the dour Belichick, a secretive sort of genius
who hated to lose, reeling,
not believing what he had seen.

That day in Arizona,
the Giants were full of fight.

The game grew old, with the Patriots trailing.
All eyes turned to Brady,
who summoned all his tricks and clicked
with Moss to regain the lead.
The climb to the top of football's Everest,
with a 19-0 record, was in their grasp.
They had delivered a knockout blow!

That day in Arizona,
the Giants were full of fight.

With the clock running down,
Tyree became the man of the hour.
He wove a pattern deep into the Patriots' lair,
Eli's arm sent a high wobbler far down field
as Tyree, at destiny's door, reached for the sky
and corralled the ball, hugging it into his helmet.
What a catch! The Hail Mary of all Hail Marys!

That day in Arizona,
the Giants were full of fight.

Eli! Eli! Eli! the crowd chanted
as if imploring a biblical character
to answer the call for a miracle.
With 35 seconds to go, Eli pitched a perfect strike
into the arms of a reawakened Burress,
battered and injured, who cried for joy
and thanked the Spirit within in him for his skill.

That day in Arizona,
the Giants were full of fight.

Proud Coughlin, proud Strahan, proud Eli, proud Tyree
had cut the string that kept the Patriots aloft for so long.
Up the Canyon of Heroes they rode,
champions of all they purviewed.
Their defense had carried them
over the hump, the perilous terrain
where once Brady's Bunch had displayed
an almost invincible perfection.

That day in Arizona,
the Giants were full of fight.

PUMPKIN SEEDS

There's an art involved in eating pumpkin seeds,
and it's best displayed in the dugouts
of baseball teams by the players
sitting on the bench waiting
their turns at bat.

They develop an indelicate precision,
a habit of spewing the shells so deftly
-- oh, it's so hard to describe -- but so plainly
understood when seen in person
or viewed on television.

It seems boorish and uncivilized
to sit there spewing mouthfuls
of pumpkin seeds onto the dugout floor,
where nobody bothers to clean them up
until the game is over and the paid attendant
does the dirty work like the latrine orderly
used to do in the Army.

It's a game within a game.
Spud, a pinch-hitter who doesn't know
if or when he'll get into the game, says
to Rusty, a substitute catcher,
"Betcha a buck, I can spit farther than you this time."
"You're on," says Rusty. "You got to get up early
to outspit me. I was Little League champ."
The spitting match begins and draws a crowd:
every ballplayer worth his salt wants a shot at it.

Spitting contests started back in the day
when players chewed tobacco and let loose
huge splatters of saliva, and chewed bubble gum,
two packs at a time, and blew bubbles

as big as baseballs and bet a few bucks
on who was the best at it. But they always
seemed to like the pumpkin seeds best.

They got so good, they could call the play,
spit a curveball, a fastball, a blooper or a home run.
This spitting business is peculiar to baseball.
I don't know why, maybe it's the slower pace
of the game -- unlike football, basketball, hockey—
where the tempo is faster and busier.

One player suggested that eating pumpkin seeds
was good for the heart and led to romance.
But what happens to romance
when you expectorate the shells
all over the place?
"Then, I guess, " the player said,
"you learn to swallow them, too."

September 2007 marked the 35th anniversary of the death of the poet Marianne Moore, winner of the Pulitzer Prize and many other prestigious awards. A protege of William Carlos Williams, she loved writing poems about baseball, too. This is a salute to her.

BATTING FOURTH, MARIANNE MOORE

I

Marianne Moore never played shortstop,
but she was a slick fielder.

She could play any position she chose
because she had sure hands

and was savvy about all things baseball.
Her strongest position, of course,

was writing poetry, great poetry,
besides the stuff on baseball.

Graceful images
of Snider and DiMaggio,

cavorting in the outfield,
dripped easily from her pen

and the pitching craftiness
of Ford and Arroyo

.

fattened her rhymes even more.
She never let a hard-hit chance get by

.

and could scoop up an errant throw
and wrap a lovely spin around it

with a few enduring words.

She saw poetry in motion
when Mantle or Mays

made a wild catch
with almost ghostlike skill.

She was deft on a fast 6 to 4 to 3 double play
initiated by the incomparable Reese,

and she perceived the magnificence
of a play at home as Robinson

slid in for a steal
or Campanella or Berra

put the tag on a chesty runner
barreling in from third, trying to score.

II

The Dodgers are long gone
from the New York scene,

where Moore lived into her old age
and died in 1972.

With regret, she saw the Dodgers
abandon Brooklyn for L.A.,

where every spring
the Bums still scamper out

to face the multitudes.
Baseball is different now

from when Moore, in stately
tricorn hat,

enjoyed the ballpark trappings
and imparted her wisdom

of the game, sculpting words
that kept even Preacher Roe

enthralled and made
Leo Durocher shut his lip

because a gentle lady
with a quill in hand

had just slammed a home run.

STEROIDS AND EGGS

Barry Bonds needed steroids and spent
millions to cultivate a habit
which would enable him to surpass
Hank Aaron's home run record.

Aaron worked on three squares a day
to keep his strength up so he could
surpass Babe Ruth's record,
although he never hit 50 in a season.

Aaron spread his clouts out
in rhythmic good measure.
The Babe surpassed all others in his time,
his records standing for many years

until Maris, McGuire, Sosa and Bonds
had the effrontery to take his place
as Sultan of Swat and give
the asterisk new importance.

McGuire and Sosa dined
at the same candy store
where Bonds ingested
his uppers and downers.

Maris relied on three squares a day.
The Babe? Well, the Babe was different.
In his inimitable fashion, he did it all on:

"Hot dogs and beer, and six eggs a day."

You can check it out with Linda Torelli,
the Babe's granddaughter.

Count Your Blessings

SPRINGSTEEN IN TRENTON

Steve flew up from Florida for Thanksgiving determined to find tickets to the last concert by The Boss on his one-man tour that would end in Trenton. Steve is tough and never admits to defeat. So he searched the Internet for hours until he landed a pair so he could take his Dad to see this great entertainer. Dad had never seen The Boss perform in person, but Steve had taught him enough through records about the hold the singer had on the American consciousness. A working man's troubadour, a Sinatra in jeans and a guitar and a harmonica. Steve had seen more Springsteen concerts than he has fingers and toes. You couldn't put one past him. There had been other troubadours: Joel, and Dylan, and Croce, and Taylor, and the fellow who sang about getting on a Jet plane, but they were nothing compared to The Boss, the man from Jersey, the real thing. Springsteen, half Irish, half Italian, a child of the melting pot.

Steve rented a truck; somehow for The Boss a truck was most appropriate. After all, wasn't he of the working, laboring poor, of blue collars and jeans, scruffy and a little raw around the edges? A Jersey poet, like Whitman! A truck was the right symbol for the lyrical, moody songs about hometown, and being born in the USA and dancing in the dark and Santa's coming to town, and hundreds of other songs of lament and melancholy that cried for justice, fair play, love and honor and the everlasting arms of Jesus.

So Steve and his Dad, an old man now and packing a cane, climbed into the truck and off they went to Trenton, capital of the state of New Jersey, a decrepit town with an arena just as

134

decrepit where 10,000 fans packed the seats in the balcony and on the floor where college teams played basketball and The Boss booked the final concert of his tour so the hometown folks could have a chance to see and hear him. The drive up the Jersey Pike was uneventful until long lines appeared at the entrance to the arena. The truck might be deprived of parking space and Dad might be shut out from seeing The Man. Steve's unwillingness to admit to defeat popped up again. He deftly swerved the truck around as if it were a bike, sped up a few yards, and drove right over the grassy divider into the next lane, which was free of traffic. Dad shouted, "Holy shit!" Steve found a place to park, and they headed for the arena. Dad limped along and happily mingled with the young at heart.

The seats were good. The show began and the famous little man came on stage and began to sing and the crowd loved what they heard. Dad felt good sitting alongside Steve, remembering his son's growing up and how he loved the G.I. Joe dolls and the racing cars in the basement and how he hit two home runs in a game on the high school team. Springsteen sang a melancholy song, and Dad grew a little sad. Dad was grateful to Steve for including him in his trip to see The Boss. The concert was magnificent and Dad was so impressed he shouted "Bravo! Bravo!" after Springsteen sang a new mournful song about a Mexican border crossing that ended in death. Dad was happy he had seen and heard Steve's musical hero and, as if in triumph, he said, "I don't give a Bravo to just anyone."

JOHNNIE TWENTY-THREE

Who would have thought he would be a Pope?
A man of peasant stock and visage.
To be a Pope, they said, you needed the O.K.
from the rich, the learned, the intelligentia.

His wealth was accumulated by simple faith:
a man of large girth and protruding nose,
the map of Italy indelibly etched in his face,
a gentle soul waiting to be chosen, anointed.

Angelo Roncalli, Johnny Twenty-Three!
A people's Pope who would open the windows
and let in the exhilarating fresh air of faith,
a worldly, compassionate Pope for all nations.

Architect of a new way, a risorgimento.
eradicator of the Catholic stain, the phrase
"perfidious Jews," from the mass
that had bound a billion souls to an ancient lie.

A toiler in the ruins of war and diplomacy,
he came to the papacy already old but wise,
gathering all his flock for a new beginning,
a conclave of new ideas and Christian unity.

Brief was his reign. but its brevity brought
joy and generosity, the spirit of ecumenism,
into a church yearning to unshackle itself
from old impediments and soiled hopes.

From peasant stock to regal son he rose
to a place among the moon and the stars.
Had he been allowed to stay with us longer
what a wondrous absolution we might have savored.

GEORGE DE GREGORIO

WILLIAM CARLOS WILLIAMS

Poet of small town America, poet of the world.
Doctor and poet, healer of bodies, healer of souls.
Buried over 40 years ago in his hometown soil of New Jersey
where Washington camped and revolutionary soldiers died.

"If you can bring nothing to this place, but carcass, keep out,"
he wrote in "Dedication for a Plot of Ground," admonishing
student and citizen alike to learn his credo.
Some of his works reside in the tiny library
across from the house where he lived.

What did the great poet see now, far from the streets of London,
Leipzig and Paris? What influence of the unsavory expatriate
Ezra Pound (sitting on the stoop at 9 Ridge Road)
penetrated his mind as he struggled with cane in hand
outside his landmark house in the twilight of a winter's day?

Like Grant at Galena, he awaited his chance at the gold ring.
Strokes had slowed him, but could not take away his dignity
or the jaunty angle at which he placed his well-worn felt hat.
Like the rest of us, he owed one death and sought peace with it.

When he put down his stethoscope at night, he sat down
to create the epic *Paterson* — like Faulkner in Yoknapatawpha,
he embraced the ethnicity that swirled about him and gave
voice and sound, smell and meaning to a swelling diversity.

Prizes came posthumously, but he did not strive for prizes.
His dream-works were built on sterner stuff—
a world-wide audience – even an audience of one or two
in the hardware store where he stopped for a daily chat.

On good days in the spring when flowers bloomed
and he no longer tended to his patients, you might see

137

the pediatrician-poet gazing at passing cars and school kids,
waiting for the sun to set, in Rutherford.

GEORGE DE GREGORIO

MATISSE IN THE MUSEUM – 2005

Matisse was ill, old and feeble when he began again
to dabble with cloth fabric and cutting out paper shapes
of things that looked, at first, like aimless images.
It was a medium he had mastered at an early age.

Now he had lost the touch that turned his oils to magic
and blazed his canvases with the fire of colors
so sublime that even Picasso made peace with him
and marveled at the brilliance and manifestations of genius.

Age wears everybody out. What is left is an imprint,
a trace of what was. For a great artist, when the brush
and the hand can no longer obey and perform,
the loss cannot be measured and he is impoverished.

For most the loss is a death knell and all that lingers
are faint aromas and fuzzy visions of the labor.
To embrace another medium, foreign and clumsy,
would be too great a leap of faith.

Throw in the towel, you who have lost your skills!
"Nonsense!" Matisse cries out from the confinement
of his bed and armchair and the strangling impotence
of illness after surgery for abdominal cancer.

He had worked too long and hard to give in
to infirmities. He would take up again with fabrics,
paper, cloth and glue to strike anew, give rebirth
to his art and reawaken long dormant dreams.

At the great museum in New York, the .master's work
was on display once again for one more show.
Matisse triumphed anew, not just in glorious canvases,
but in the revelation of his early genius for blending

139

cloth, synthetic fabrics and paper into myriad shapes and colors that draped and refurbished all his works.

GEORGE DE GREGORIO

A SPECIAL SON

*(A tribute to James Suozzo, son of the author's life-long friend
and college roommate)*

In the measure of time,
he was gone in the blinking of an eye.
Gone even before the completion
of the life cycle of his parents.
Harshest blow of all, unnatural,
yet joyous in its brevity.

A widow and five sons left behind
amid a throng of broken hearts,
friends and family, all grieving
for the life-force, so strong,
so loving, snuffed out so soon,
just as it had become acquainted
with the mystery, the beauty
that brims the cup of life
and gives to Man the stature
of the healer and peacemaker.

Something in his spirit showed the way,
an inner depth, perhaps meant for a mission
as a preacher administering to a flock
in need of love and care and inner strength.
A prophet, snatched away at 46, trailing
a glory of laughter and good feeling.

Flowers strewn around his coffin, petals
of warmth and love in such abundance
they made his path to heaven
a garden of unquenchable beauty.
O the sweetness, O the honor, O the love
for such an ordinary human man.

His gift was bridging the great racial divide
to be the father of five sons whose seed,
entwined with his and his mate's, brought
forth a blend of handsome strength and fidelity,
laughter and hope for the future of all men.
"Do not grieve for me," James would have said.
Rather think of him alive alongside each of us,
laughing, enjoying good times,
knowing he loved us all as we loved him
and how wonderful he thought it was to be among us.

JAMES BALDWIN CAME BACK HOME

From the broiling Harlem streets, the little black boy,
odd-looking in the first place, took abuse
from other black boys and wondered why
he could not get refuge and comfort
at least from his step-father, a fire-and-brimstone minister.

His birth father had flown the coop
and left James naked and unprotected
from the taunts and physical abuse
inflicted in the neighborhood.

Racism had many faces, it wasn't always white
against black, black against white, or yellow,
or brown, or red, or all the colors of the rainbow.
Back in the day, racial profiling came right out
without camouflage, naked and unadorned:
"Black boy, black boy, spin around, little black Sambo
        is in town."

Imagine reading a children's book in kindergarten
about Little Black Sambo chasing
a tiger and melting into butter!
For James Baldwin, racism was real and painful—
an everyday occurrence, with a twist entirely different
from the common, accepted brand. The streets of Harlem
produced enough hatred from black-on-black racism

to go round the world, even before it sprouted
between black and white in the American North and South
and in Africa, blighting and disgracing entire nations.
James Baldwin came to this contradiction
in the marrow of his bones, long before the powder keg blew up.

Go tell it on the mountain! He proclaimed.

ZERILDA'S CHAIR AND OTHER POEMS

The fire next time! The fire next time! —
mantras warning all within earshot
of a coming tide of bitter and unreasonable strife —
even as the world staggered from Fascistic hatred.

Even if the world lasted another 2,000 years,
racism and its scars, might never heal.
Had James Baldwin lived until 2009,
he would have seen Barack Obama, a black man,
take office as President of the United States,
a milestone so gigantic and yet so simple and logical
it might wipe hate from the hearts of men or feed on it more
ravenously so it might never go away.

Did James Baldwin have a role in this emergence of freedom?
Was his international escape from dark Harlem,
where riots and killings erupted from sun-up to sundown,
shove him into the arms of the gay streets of Paris
where sex and drugs became his refuge?

Did his disillusion with American racism become a crutch,
hiding him from the reality waging in his native land?
Baldwin became so attached to the black man's
struggle for equality, and yearning for love and beauty,
that he could not stay away from his native soil.

He returned from Paris to engage
in the erupting civil rights battle,
heading South with his friends,
Martin and Malcolm and Jesse,
hoping to join the struggle
which would liberate his people.

"Let freedom ring!" shouted Martin,
and James heard the cry and knew
he had to come back home.

NODDING IN SILENCE

I am not a celebrity-watcher,
but bumping into one by accident
on an elevator has a certain charm.
Itzak Perlman. a magnificent artist,
left me in awe one day as I rode
with him when I worked at *The New York Times*
in the old building on West 43rd Street.
It was a quiet jaunt to the 11^{th-}floor cafeteria.
We were the only passengers.
We nodded in silence.

He was aware that I knew who he was.
No need to try to be overly friendly.
I noticed a constant twinkle in his eyes,
as if he were talking to someone,
or visualizing a score he was playing on his violin.

His calmness and the strength
he seemed to exude made an impression
as he stood with his braces and walking canes,
his shoulders as massive
and wide as any linebacker's;
his strong-looking neck supporting a huge head,
with a handsome shock of graying hair.
When I got off at the 11th, he stayed on.

JUST A FEW WORDS MORE

(A prose poem, read on a special occasion marking 50 years of marriage)
Williamsburg, Virginia
June 16, 1956 to June 16, 2006
To Barry, Steven, Karen, Carl, Marcia, Zachary, Abigail, Emily:

I want to say just a few words on this golden celebration
and I hope your mother will second them and you will

not object to them. There aren't many couples who can say
they have remained married for 50 years, but your Dad,

also known as Grandpa D., and your mother , also known
as Grandma D., have managed to pull it off – with the help

of God, a lot of sweat, a lot of angst and tears and, most of all,
with a lot of love. No marriage can last for 50 years without help

and a strong commitment to make it work.
Of course, it had to start with a solid foundation.
Your Mom, who carried the brunt of caring

for your daily needs while I was off to work, is the rock
for that foundation. She and I believe love is the greatest force

on earth. I hope she will forgive me for presuming to speak
for her, but in my heart I know she shares that generosity.

When I was young I served in the Army and went to Japan.
I had easy duty because the war had ended. I was attached

to a medical unit and I learned to give immunization shots
to soldiers and civilians. It was a great experience.

GEORGE DE GREGORIO

On my desk I always kept a little reminder,
a paper with a quotation from a famous judge
whom I admired in those days.

He talked about the Spirit of Liberty, something I think
we should all admire. The place we are in today, celebrating

this golden event, has a lot to do with remembering that spirit...
Judge Learned Hand wrote: ...

*"The spirit of liberty remembers that not even a sparrow falls to
earth unheeded. The spirit of liberty is the spirit of Him who
nearly 2,000 years ago, taught mankind that lesson it has never
learned, but has never quite forgotten: that there may be a
kingdom where the least shall be heard and considered side by
side with the greatest."*

Dear wonderful children, your Mom and I are proud
of all you have done, and pray that you will continue to be wise,

stubborn if need be, thoughtful of others, strong in pursuing
your bliss and believe deeply in what is worthwhile

to attain happiness for yourselves now and in the future.
Love one another and may God bless you all.

Mom (Grandma D.) and Dad (Grandpa D.)
Barbara and George